The Pillars of Unitism

Daniel H. Crawford III

The Pillars of Unitism
2

The Pillars of Unitism

1)   Section One: Introduction
a)   Chapter 1: Brief Autobiography
b)   Chapter 2: History of Unitism
c)   Chapter 3: Corruptive Nature of Money in Politics
2)   Section Two: Justice and Security
a)   Chapter 4: International Protection
b)   Chapter 5: National Protection
c)   Chapter 6: Local Protection
3)   Section Three: Science
a)   Chapter 7: Environmentalism
b)   Chapter 8: Controversial Medical Research
c)   Chapter 9: Evolution
d)   Chapter 10: Agnosticism and Secularism
4)   Section Four: Human Rights
a)   Chapter 11: Basic Freedoms and Rights
b)   Chapter 12: The Right to Choose (Abortion)
c)   Chapter 13: The Right to Die (Euthanasia)
5)   Section Five: Economics
a)   Chapter 14: Healthcare
b)   Chapter 15: Retirement
c)   Chapter 16: Social Democracy
d)   Chapter 17: Marxism
6)   Section Six: Politics
a)   Chapter 18: Democracy
b)   Chapter 19: The Accompaniment Theory
c)   Chapter 20: Choosing Our Path

The Pillars of Unitism
4

Section One: Introduction

Chapter One: Brief Autobiography

Chapter One: Brief Autobiography

I was born in Fort Riley, Kansas to two people whose views on life couldn't have been further from each other. On the one hand, you have my father. He's a very conservative person who has religiously listened to talk radio throughout the course of his two decades as a truck driver. His service in the military is obviously the reason that I was born in Fort Riley, and also influenced the fact that my two sisters were born in Germany.

Then, you have my mother. As a moderately-liberal person, this woman's heart was big enough to fit the Empire State Building in it. She had long desired to enter the medical field and become a nurse, but health problems – as will be discussed later – hindered her from realizing such dreams. Never content with hearing information from one source, she always made it a point to try and research an issue a little more before reaching a conclusion. Needless to say, the internet was her best friend when the World Wide Web became so easily navigable.

At an early age – my toddler years, to be exact -, I had to become accustomed to moving around a lot. My earliest memories are from when we lived in Germany – which was from 1986 to 1989 -, and those are mostly good memories. I remember the airplane trip back, during which our plane flew either over or near Hurricane Hugo as we landed in Florida. We actually had to briefly sleep in the terminal – which I remember, because I looked out the window at the planes as it was raining and storming heavily outside - before we secured a hotel room whereat we enjoyed pizza and a King Kong movie.

From there, we eventually made our way to Kansas again where we mostly lived in trailer parks before buying a house. I developed a fear for tornadoes later in life as an indirect consequence of our time there, but was oddly entertained by them at the time. After selling our house for a pathetically-low price – a fact that my mother never stopped complaining about -, we moved to the state of my parents' birth: Ohio, which is where I've lived ever since. After that point, we spent the 1990s never staying in any one place for more than two years. This would later lead me to start telling people that we were Nomads when I learned what they were in the Fourth Grade.

In 1992, five years after the birth of my youngest sister – and seven years after me -, the fourth and final child was born into my family. Seen as being some kind of god-send for their failing marriage, my brother became a sign of new hope and unity for my parents. To us, his three eldest siblings, the birth of this child was an exciting change. Helping Mom with diaper changes, bottle feeding, and encouraging him to crawl was made to be a lot of fun.

Over the course of our childhood, my siblings and I developed a close relationship. Sure, we had our knock-down, drag-out fights, but our bond was as close as one would come to expect with kids born in a cluster like we were. We played together, laughed together, and struggled together. Life wasn't always peachy, and perhaps I'm using rose-tinted glasses here in my hindsight, but some of the best lessons I learned in life were from growing up with three of my favorite people on the face of the Earth.

Some of those lessons dealt with survival, as our family experienced homelessness for about two or three weeks in the early fall of 1993 after a roommate of ours pointed a gun at my Mom one day, thus prompting her to decide that we would be better off moving out even if we didn't have anywhere else to go at that moment. At first, we lived in a tent on a campground for the bulk of that time. To us kids, this was yet another adventure, and it provided us with the opportunity to meet a number of really nice people. It got weird, though, when all the other camping families gradually left the grounds. The five of us sleeping closely every night in our collection of sleeping bags, hearing coyotes at night, the cold baths via gallon jugs of unheated water, and the daily removal of ticks is an experience I will not soon forget.

With fall starting to kick in, my Mother had finally had enough. She refused to let her kids deal with this for another day, so she did what any loving mother in her position would do; she took us to a house and broke in. Don't be alarmed, for the house she broke into belonged to her parents. You see, they were trapped in Missouri by the Great Flood of that year, and we only stayed for a few days until my Mom secured a new home for us to live in. Until her dying day, though she knew it was the right thing to do, she never forgave herself for violating the trust of my grandparents like that.

Sadly, that was only the first in a series of struggles. Within a few months, my Father left my Mother – informing her of his desire for a divorce via a letter in the mail – and we were again left in the cold as our inability to pay the gas bill led to a freezing house, everyone sleeping in one bed, a number of bouts wherein all three of us older kids were afflicted with a vicious cold, and eventually

my Mother deciding that we would move in with a coworker. Due to that decision,

the summer of 1994 will always be one of the worst in my lifetime, as this new

roommate turned out to be a monster who hated children.

From force-feeding and beating my toddler brother senseless to locking

us kids out of the house during the daylight, this horrible abusive woman took

advantage of the fact that my Mother worked and went to school almost every day.

Eventually, there were three families living in that house; which, as I was told, was

an old mansion from the Nineteenth Century. There were roughly fifteen or so

people living together, and the situation only got worse. When the fall came, us

kids and a teenage roommate revealed the horrors of our daily life to my Mother,

and she again uprooted us as we left all of our belongings behind – all of which the

monster later sold – and headed for a battered woman's shelter one county over.

We weren't there long, but it was strange living in a place into which you

basically had to sneak. I had to tell one friend of mine from school that he couldn't

follow me home because our location was supposed to remain a secret. Also, I was

particularly annoyed with the fact that watching shows like "Power Rangers" was

forbidden – due to the violence -, but I guess that I now understand why that was

the case. Thankfully, we saw some semblance of stability returning to our lives

when we moved into a new house of our own.

As a single mother, Mom worked most of her days away as the position

of Nurse's Aid can often be a demanding job. Even so, life was becoming

enjoyable once more. Mom even met a new and interesting fellow who was "legally blind", played funny songs on his acoustic guitar, and had three boys of

his own. This man would become her second husband who she never stopped

loving, even after they had a bitter divorce five years later. The intervening years

were more fun than not, involving a family business, camping trips, and the

introduction of a family tradition celebrating New Years in style.

I mentioned before my Mother's hardworking nature, a key part of her

character which was probably inspired by the same characteristic found in her

father. She would tell us kids about how she would only see him on the weekends,

because of how his work hours were scheduled. To be honest, I'm not sure if he

realizes how much she idolized him. His devotion to providing for his family was

the standard of parenting to which she held herself every day. This is both a good

and bad thing, as she never felt that she had fully fulfilled her role.

At some point after marrying her second husband, she became unable to

work in Nursing – since the work and other health issues were steadily wearing

her down -, and the newlywed couple opened their own cleaning business within a

few months. Though there were some tasks that were too dangerous for us kids to

help in, Mom made it a point to involve all of us. It was a lot of fun helping clean

restaurants and offices, and we were learning important lessons about the

workforce. Those were good times, but they only lasted a few years, as the end of

the business became one of several factors in the end of the marriage.

When I was fifteen, my mom made me get a job. She didn't make me

give her any of the money I made, but she was determined to make sure that I

learned something valuable about work ethic. In her eyes, working in your teens –

as she had done – was crucial to becoming a responsible adult. With the exception

of a year or two of total accumulated time between jobs, I've worked ever since.

Honestly, I'm grateful for those values, as they have led me to make

tough workforce-based decisions when I got married and had two children of my

own. Had it not been for her insistence that I work when I didn't want to, I don't

know how compelled I would have been to abandon bad jobs for better ones when

the opportunity presented itself. The reason I say this is that I tend to like staying

where I am, as change in some respects creates too much confusion.

Either way, her dedication as a parent continues to inform my decisions

along the same lines every day. Of course, parenthood itself changes you anyways.

Ever since the birth of my son in 2006, my perspective on life has transformed. I

no longer look at society through the lens of my own eyes, but through a crystal

ball which projects how current events will impact the lives of my children and

grandchildren. In essence, parenthood can make one a more socially involved and

concerned animal.

Life lessons are considerably different as an adult as compared to when

you are a child. The burden of worrying belongs solely to the parent, and when life

rapidly changes it is the adult in the situation who absorbs the full weight of the

world as it collapses upon them. This reality became fully apparent to me from

2009 through 2012 as my family endured one crisis after another. First, my

employer forced me to switch from one contract to another paying more than a

dollar less per hour. Then, a year later, further cutbacks initially cut me down from

full-time to part-time followed by a layoff within a week's time.

After a month of working for a temp service, I was left unemployed for ten months after that temp assignment suddenly came to an end. The unemployment only ended when I gave up looking for a full-time job and settled for working as a temp for about a year and a half before finally landing a part-time position as a cashier at a local grocery store. Needless to say, I have come to appreciate my mother for maintaining her sanity in having to provide for four children largely by herself; especially considering how inconsistent the child-support payments were.

I'm proud to say that I did one thing that my mother was never able to – by no fault of her own -; earn a college degree. Mom was very supportive both times that I pursued a college degree. The first time, for reasons to be tackled shortly, I dropped out after a few months despite having great grades and being placed on the Dean's List. When I went back to school roughly three years later, the significant pay cut I just mentioned had taken effect. To put it lightly, I was desperate to escape this unstable lifestyle and to provide a better life for my kids than what I had lived. After she passed away in May 2012 – on my father and stepfather's birthday -, I dedicated my degree in Political Science and Government to my mother's memory.

On the flipside, the combination of my two attempts at a college education left me with a mountain of intimidating debt. Shortly after I got married in 2007, I idiotically allowed myself to default on my student loans from the first round of school. Needless to say, that was the last time I will ever allow that to happen. Going back to school as an adult is good for society overall, but the debt

that such incurs for those without connections is a significant hurdle to overcome.

Back to my mom, when we lost her, it was a cruel ending to a prolonged

and tragic decline. Born to a mother with Type 1 Diabetes, and a member of a

family with a history of cancer, she was almost destined to develop health issues.

In 1994 it was discovered that she had an autoimmune disease, then – in 1997 –

she had to have her gall bladder removed. Soon thereafter the doctors found cancer

in her thyroid; which was removed in the Spring of 1998.

As it turns out, the fact that she was exposed to the fallout from

Chernobyl in Northern Europe when she was pregnant with my oldest sister may

have had a big part to play. Her health progressively worsened at an ever-

accelerating rate throughout the 1990s. Despite the fact that she enjoyed exercise,

worked hard, and largely avoided junk food, she gained a frightening amount of

weight. It was our hope that the cancerous thyroid's removal would help her get

back to normal, but we were wrong.

At some point within a year or so of the surgery, Mom started receiving

the wrong dosage for the medicine meant to replace the thyroid's function in

distinguishing between good and bad fat. So, the weight gain was only

exacerbated from there. Within three years, she was rendered disabled as the

weight – in conjunction with the physical consequences of working as a Nurse's

Aid – took its toll on her spine. No matter how much she wanted to, walking had

become far too excruciating for her to do so regularly.

It is inspiring to me how she still never gave up, even with everything working against her. She was never content to hear one Doctor's opinion, nor would she take "no" for an answer when she pleaded for help. After all, to her, she had to keep fighting for the sake of the four children who depended on and cherished her so much. Later on, as she was crying out for mercy and for a chance to live a normal and productive life once again, I joined her campaign to secure what would have been a life-saving gastric bypass operation. The reason that this campaign was necessary was that a medical decision in the spring of 2005 deemed "obesity" as a lifestyle choice, which meant that all operations pertaining to such were determined to be "elective"; therefore, Medicaid wouldn't cover such.

Publicly dubbing it "Operation Save Mom", I contacted elected officials at each level of government and begged them to do whatever they could. Congressman Ney stepped up, Governor Taft looked into it, our State Representative contacted Medicaid, our Mayor contacted the Ohio State University's Medical Center, and a number of City Council members answered the plea as well. Eventually, the local paper caught wind of our efforts – perhaps after I had submitted a special guest column to same said paper – and did a story on us. Unfortunately, the story was worded in a way which made it seem like we were asking for help with Christmas.

Yes, we appreciated the good-hearted nature of the community's response in that respect, but the only real gift that my family wanted was for our Mother to get the help she so desperately needed. We wanted her to live, but when the public's holiday compassion came and went, she continued to suffer for another six and a half years. In 2009, it was finally discovered that she had developed

uterine cancer. By then, it was too late, as the hysterectomy and the two grueling

years of chemotherapy and radiation treatments merely mangled what was left of

this incredible woman until she was permanently bed-ridden and left to die in a

nursing home a little more than two weeks after her 49th birthday.

My life story isn't all tragedy and trials, though. Having a mother like

mine also came with some valuable perks, with one of those being the sense of

duty to others she helped instill in me. This important part of life was first taught

to me via my initial Christian upbringing. Mom was a devout believer – though,

not a bible-thumper by any stretch of the imagination -, and set out to teach us kids

both how to read the Bible and how to apply its lessons about mercy, love, and

compassion to our fellow human beings. It was always my impression that Mom's

faith in the notion of "what comes around, goes around" was reinforced by what

may have been her favorite part of the Bible: the golden rule.

Before I understood anything else in the Bible, I knew what it meant to

"do onto others". In fact, my mother practiced this every day of her life. As long as

she had something to give for the benefit of someone in need you can guarantee

that she was giving. I grew up seeing her welcome strangers in our home to offer

them a bite to eat, giving money to people in desperate need, even letting people

live with us from time to time. Sure, there were instances where people would take

advantage of her charitable ways, but that fact never deterred her willingness to

lend a helping hand.

Seeing her example, and in taking the golden rule seriously, I started to mimic her actions. When I was sixteen, I was approached by a homeless man who asked if I could spare some money. Without hesitation, I reached into my pockets and dug up all the change I could find and handed it to him. His gleeful reaction lit a fire inside me, and I continued to repeat this every time I was asked to help by a homeless person for the next few years. I didn't care what they were using the money for, because that was their concern. The only thing I knew is that this was a new kind of satisfaction; I loved helping people.

In a way, it is probably this fact that I so thoroughly enjoyed the feeling of helping when I could that led me to scoff at the thought of people being so selfish when reacting to programs such as food stamps and Medicaid. With a few exceptions during better times, I grew up and started a family of my own with the government being there to help in one way or another. I'm thankful that society – through these assistance programs – was there for my family when we needed them. There is no shame in seeking help, nor is there any shame in helping.

I can not deny the conditioning of my duty to others by my early religiosity, my mother's example, or by the help from the taxpayers. However, as an adult, the basis for this duty to serve the interests of humanity has evolved alongside my beliefs. In college, I learned of a rational basis for serving others during my first ethics-based course. With utilitarianism, deontology, and John Rawls's "veil of ignorance", one could justify having a heart without religion. As will be discussed further in the next chapter, my conversion to Agnosticism was partially aided by this very liberation of my need to show compassion.

So, there you have it, the story of my life. It is my hope that this chapter has helped to explain why it is that I have chosen to write this book. Now, we will explore the history of this political theory and ideology: Unitism.

Section One: Introduction

Chapter Two: History of Unitism

Chapter Two: History of Unitism
Exposure to Politics: From Childhood to Present

My love of and interest in politics originated from my initial exposure thereto. As I mentioned in the previous chapter, my mother and father were interested in politics. When I was seven years old, I remember sitting in the living room of a family friend's house as my Mother exclaimed with joy during Bill Clinton's victory speech in the 1992 election. I may not have understood what was going on, but I knew that it made my Mom happy. Due to the personal chaos mentioned before, I didn't pay attention to another election until 1996.

On election night in that Presidential Election, my sixth grade history teacher gave us an assignment wherein we had to take home an electoral map and keep track of the election results. Needless to say, I was amazed at how easily Clinton won that night; with more than 370 electoral votes! This caught me off guard mostly because my elementary school had held a mock election a few weeks earlier and had produced a much closer end result; though, Clinton still won. Moreover, the 1996 contest produced an initial fascination with the Electoral College – as well as with politics overall -, as it appeared to be simple and fair.

Honestly, the next two or three years only enhanced my political interest. Indeed, it was confusing to have this president of whom I had become quite fond accused of and eventually confess to an extramarital affair, but the impeachment process was a new learning experience for yours truly. Again, I was enamored by the world of politics, only now I found myself glued to the television, especially as CSPAN covered the impeachment process itself. Of course, no political event had a greater influence on my future activism than the next presidential election.

Now in High School, I had heard a great deal about the then-impending contest. It was obvious to me in the Spring of 2000 that George W. Bush was going to square off against Al Gore that fall. On Election Night, Mom and I had bought snacks and drinks in preparation for a party of sorts, but we had no idea that there would be no winner that night. I stayed up as late as I could watching the coverage and was astounded when I awoke the next morning to the news that we were still without a winner.

To this date, I still have the calendar from that year which was marked with personal notes about important dates pertaining to the recount. When, in December, the Supreme Court stepped in and handed Bush the White House, I was beside myself. Suffice it to say, that I was no longer a fan of the Electoral College after that, and was determined to see the removal of Bush from the office that he undoubtedly stole. In keeping up to date, watching cable news and reading internet-based news became a daily obsession.

You can imagine how excited I was to turn eighteen in 2003. I no longer had to watch these major events from the sidelines. As soon as I could, I registered to vote, and began watching the Democratic Presidential Debates of that year. Eventually, I became acquainted with my local party headquarters and happily voted for the first time in the local election in November; rejoicing when my choice for Mayor came out the victor.

In 2004, I had completed my transition into activism. From my enthusiastic support for Dennis Kucinich during the primaries to my frequent volunteering during the general campaign after the Democratic Convention, I was entirely consumed by the effort to unseat Bush. A couple of weeks before John

Kerry visited my hometown, the local paper even published a letter of mine as a

guest column entitled "Christians stand behind Kerry"; talk about an ego booster! I

had also grown fond of campaign buttons, as I wore them literally everywhere I

went.

On Election Day, I was extremely confident that Kerry was going to win.

I went home and prepared for a night of celebration, especially since we – at the

local campaign headquarters – had been told that exit polls in Virginia, Florida,

and Ohio were leaning heavily in our favor. Knowing that I had to be at work at

six in the morning, I took a nap. Upon waking up, I started to see the night take a

turn for the worst with each of the aforementioned battlegrounds flipping against

Kerry. By the end of the night, my entire household was in tears, fearing what the

next four years held.

Despite the disappointment of 2004, the local party remained a

rejuvenated force, and almost swept all the local elections the following year.

Then, our sights were set on 2006 and winning control of Congress. Gradually

getting back into the habit of volunteering again, I had a chance to have a few

enlightening conversations with our candidates that year; including a five minute

discussion with future Governor – and then-Congressman – Ted Strickland about

the need to impeach Bush and a series of conversations with future Congressman

Zack Space along the same lines. Unlike the previous national elections from 2000

through 2004, the results of 2006 left me with a renewed sense of optimism about

the future.

I will admit that I was not on the Obama bandwagon at first. In 2007, I had once again found myself rooting for Kucinich, and I was more militant about the impeachment issue during that year than ever before. Speaker Pelosi, Congressman Space, and Barack Obama's insistence that Bush and Cheney's removal be left "off the table" was unacceptable to me. Not even considering the perfectly constitutional remedy for the Administration's egregious abuses of power was unconscionable and a constant source of frustration, and Kucinich's attempts to do something about it only solidified my support for him.

Even so, I eventually came to support Obama in the primaries when Kucinich dropped out, because I did not want Hillary Clinton – who had voted to give Bush the authority to invade Iraq – to be the nominee. However, Obama lost my support for a while that summer when he voted for the deceptively-named "Protect America Act" which retroactively immunized the telecommunications industry from lawsuits for their participation in what was effectively rendered a newly-legal surveillance program. Declaring that Obama was going to merely continue Bush's abuses in the name of "fighting terror", I pledged my support for Ralph Nader. Then John McCain chose Sarah Palin as his running-mate.

In the weeks that followed, I saw and learned how insane this Alaskan Governor was, and it became obvious to me that to risk her being a "heartbeat away from the presidency" was something that I could not justify. So, I held my nose and voted for Obama. Once he actually won the election, my reluctant support turned into tearful glee. I could not help but to become emotional about this incredible achievement when I saw the tears of joy from African American supporters on my television screen; most notably, that of the Reverend Jesse Jackson.

Sadly, it didn't take long for the bitterness on the other side of the aisle to overwhelm any sense of patriotism. I'm not saying that conservatives should have just accepted President Obama's agenda, but openly hoping for him to "fail" and refusing to work with him on legislation meant to save the country from a second Great Depression didn't strike me as reasonable or – at the very least – as the conduct of people who loved their country. Moreover, the convenient political amnesia as to the origins of recent budget deficits and the exploding national debt made it hard to sympathize with a group which had been so open to reckless spending when such was not necessary during the time in which they held all the cards.

This opposition soon found a new weapon in the so-called Tea Party. Thanks to the controversial push by President Obama for a reform of the nation's healthcare system – which was largely molded by conservative ideas once advanced in the Clinton years, and which bent over backwards to ignore the views of liberals -, the Republican Party rode this wave of resentment, hate, and paranoia to a sweeping victory in a Midterm election featuring a severely depressed turnout. At that point, the stage was set for gridlock and brinksmanship which effectively promised that our government would be run from one manufactured crisis – to borrow a term from the President himself – to the next.

Yet, there remained a silver-lining in the Republican sweep of 2010; the backlash that its consequences would help produce. 2011, in many ways, became the year of democracy both at home and abroad. Kicked off internationally by the so-called Arab Spring as the people throughout that region began to push for greater control over their nation-state's affairs via wrestling the reins from long-standing tyrants, the wave of people power swept the globe. Here in America, the pro-democratic movement began in reaction to the extreme economic policies of the newly-elected Republican-controlled State Governments throughout the country; most notably those policies attacking the rights of workers to organize.

This assault on social democracy merely added another layer to wider campaign against democracy overall. Beginning in early-2010 with the now-infamous Supreme Court ruling on "Citizens United" – a ruling to be discussed further in the next chapter -, the proverbial floodgates restricting the flow of special interest money were obliterated, thus relegating our system to what can arguably be labeled a democracy-in-name-only. By the fall of 2011, this anger about the shift of influence on all fronts in our society towards the wealthiest few inspired the Occupy Wall Street movement's emergence. In recognizing the importance of this movement and how it was crucial for the citizenry to take a stand in defense of our right to popular sovereignty, I spearheaded – along with about a dozen other great people - the creation of my local region's own "Occupy" group.

Beginnings of Unitism

Truth be told, I wasn't always this patriotic or this passionate about democracy. Sadly, Unitism began on the complete opposite side of the equation. When I was ten years old, I had an unusual reaction to learning about the national anthem's history. At that age, something about boasting rubbed me the wrong

way, and I had come to feel that the anthem – which was written about a battle in

the War of 1812 – was nothing more than a chest-pounding taunt to our former

brethren in Great Britain. It didn't help matters that the art work for the anthem in

our music class looked like mythical scenes from the movie "300", thus

exacerbating my perception of a detestable display of pride.

In my elementary understanding of the world, and of my religious faith at

the time, I had interpreted the anthem and everything it celebrated as immoral. I

had convinced my young and impressionable brain that the British should have

won the Revolutionary War and that our separation from the Crown was a sign of

our moral decay. I held this viewpoint for an embarrassing period of time

afterward, though the allegiance to Britain didn't last long into my teen years.

Instead, I shifted gears from wanting to return this country to its erstwhile status as

a collection of colonies to wanting a religious doctrine at the helm.

After the 2000 election debacle caused me to lose whatever faith I had in

our democracy and after the attacks on September 11th had convinced me that the

world was going mad without God, I determined that we should convert our

Democratic Republic into a Monarchy of sorts. At the age of sixteen, I sat at my

Mother's computer for several hours and composed what I called the "Second

Declaration of Independence". Before emailing the document to hundreds of

strangers, I proposed drafting a new constitution with a legal system based entirely

off the King James Version of the Holy Bible, and a Monarchy wherein the King

and Queen would be selected by what would have been the last election, as it would have permanently installed their bloodline as our rulers. Thankfully, this

support for a Theocratic Absolute-Monarchy in America only lasted for a few

months until the Patriot Act and the push for war with Iraq convinced me that

having an all-powerful executive was definitely the wrong route.

Transformation

As can be seen throughout what this book has mentioned so far, 2004 was

a significant year for me. Among many personal twists and turns, the year marked

my first experience in working to elect a president. From July of that year until

Election Day, I regularly volunteered my efforts to try and elect John Kerry.

Phone-banking, canvassing, dropping literature at houses was a routine part of my

week. In the process, I fell in love with America and our system of governance.

Regardless of the outcome, my patriotism was kindled for the first time, and it

burns hot to this date.

However, unlike the patriots on the other end of the spectrum, my pride

was growing as both an American and as a human being. Perhaps the most

important change was in how I had ceased to see the world as a den of iniquity.

After the Kerry rally in my hometown, I found myself in a lengthy conversation

with another attendee about the impending gay marriage ban on the ballot that year

here in Ohio. I had expressed my religious-based support for the ban to which the

fellow retorted that it wasn't just going to affect same-sex couples. When he

revealed that he was actually gay I stood shocked, and found myself conflicted

about my position on that issue and on specific issues of "morality". Ultimately, when the time came to vote, I elected to reject the ban; a decision for which I am deeply proud to date.

Speaking of internal conflict over morality, 2004 sparked the beginning of a domino effect in my religious beliefs. In truth, doubts had lingered ever since I was seven or eight when I openly questioned why the dinosaurs – which was an obsession of mine at the time – were nowhere to be seen in the Bible. Then again, I had eventually been comforted by theories that the prehistoric creatures had been killed off in the Great Flood of Noah, so I was no longer vexed with such questions. 2004, though, was a year when my religiosity would peak and begin to crumble.

It started when the pastor of my church had called for all of us in attendance to take responsibility for the conversion of "one soul" to our Pentecostal beliefs. So, liking a challenge, I set out to "save" my manager at my fast food job. What made this task a challenge was the fact that this man was well-versed in scripture, as he used to be a Jehovah's Witness. Not knowing the implications of his background, I accepted his invitation to visit him at his home with my Bible and a compilation of seemingly-irrefutable passages. Much to my dismay, he was fully capable of dissecting my weak approach and taught me that my version of the Bible was littered with a number of modifications which made it different from every other version.

Feeling as if I had been fed into a wood-chipper, I went home and began to research everything that he had said. It was enraging and depressing to discover that he was completely right; the Bible I held and swore by had been altered from original scripture and had even been changed numerous times after the fact.

Everything that I had come to believe – particularly with respect to the "Rapture"

– was in doubt. Even so, I continued to attend my church through to the Spring of

2005, which was another issue in and of itself.

As a member of that church, I had been increasingly alarmed by some of

the rhetoric of its leader. For instance, the Pastor was adamant and outspoken in

his support for what he said was a "just war" in Iraq. Moreover, the Pastor made it

a point to plead with his followers that they vote for the presidential candidate

holding the "right" position on abortion. At that point, I decided that since he

brought politics into the church, I would wear my buttons supporting Kerry every

time I attended. Let's just say that harassing me for such was a favorite activity for

church members up to the first Sunday after Election Day.

I did eventually separate myself from that church, though, seeing such as

more heretical than holy. In fact, with the exception of a brief stint at a little family

church a couple houses down the block from me, I never settled into another

church. My service to Christianity was mostly observed in private, with daily

prayers and reading of my Bible, because I was determined to go about my beliefs

in the correct manner. It wasn't long before this decision to think for myself and

with an open mind began to erode my faith.

In 2008, after having tried to ignore the facts throughout my life, I finally

accepted the theories of evolution, the big bang, and the Earth's age as fact.

Science was gradually interrupting my superstition. About a year or so into my

college studies, after a world history course and an anthropology course taught me about ancient belief systems and syncretism, I seriously started to question the

logic of my continued faith. Then, in October of 2011, I reached the point where I

had to convert to agnosticism when I saw the formation of a perfect rainbow via

the setting sun's rays. At that moment – when it became clear that rainbows

existed regardless of whether or not there ever was a global flood (a belief that was

instilled in me as a child, upheld by the Bible, and which loosely held my faith

intact since I never before made the visual of the scientific explanation for a

rainbow) – I had lost all ability to deny that my faith was any more rational than

that of the old Mayans sacrificing people for the pleasure of their mythical gods.

To continue calling myself a Christian – no matter how badly I wanted to keep the

faith – would have been a truly cowardly and dishonest decision given what I had

come to realize.

Likewise, my faith in the capitalist economic system was weakened over

time. At a young age, I heard the terms "communism", "socialism", and

"capitalism" without any real understanding as to how they were different from

one another. Sure, I learned about the concept of "supply and demand", but the

only mention about the other two economic systems involved negative references

to the "defeated" Soviet Union and the Cold War. I recall nothing about Karl Marx

or his vision ever being discussed; a fact I mostly attribute to the obsession of

many history teachers to overemphasize and even glorify the periods of war while

rushing through all other topics.

Despite my lack of knowledge about the differences between the

economic approaches, I was learning all on my own just how unsustainable capitalism was. My former religious beliefs taught me to despise greed – which is a key component for capitalism -, and that alone was causing me to distrust the current system. This perception of the economy's design only got worse with every year after seeing my mother struggle to get her surgery, suffering a layoff and the personal aftermath of such, as well as watching the world's economy come crashing down in 2008. I was primed for a change, and my curiosity about socialism and communism only grew.

While I remained cautious about completely supporting socialism or communism – which were still tainted in my mind based on the examples of China and the Soviets -, I knew that capitalism itself was in trouble. It wasn't until I had been in college for a little more than a year when a political science course enlightened me as to what Marxism is as a political theory and ideology. Suddenly, it was all clear to me. Marx wasn't some political demon, but rather he was an intellectual who saw history through the lens of economic justice and fairness. Marxism wasn't meant to be an ideology of conquest or dominance, but of liberation for all from the same.

A Complete Picture

Finally, the political theory and ideology which I started to develop in 1995 at the age of 10 was showing signs of being whole. With Marx providing the final piece – a path towards a classless and selfless society -, the future looked brighter. Marxism appeals to the part of me which still resents selfishness and calls for communities to work as one. Such a world would – in theory – be devoid of needless suffering and even war. Peace on Earth would finally be attainable as

humanity worked collectively as opposed to individually.

Accompanying Marxism was my renewed and strengthened appreciation

for democracy. Having learned more about this political system in my history and

political science courses, the fact that democracy is about placing the reins of

power in the people's hands was all I needed to know. Of course, in the age of

Revolution, communication traveled too slowly, and information was too

unavailable for too many for there to be a direct democracy at America's founding.

However, advancements in education and the advent of the internet have since

demolished those former barriers to an effective pure democracy.

Lastly, my conversion from an absolutist religious viewpoint to the open-

minded agnosticism I currently observe ensured that no form of tyranny would

creep into this vision. Refusing to assume an irrational certitude about the

existence or nonexistence of a supreme being, it is my belief that a state-based

agnosticism would allow for humanity's curiosity via scientific research to find an

answer while remaining tolerant of individual religious beliefs. In this way, I feel

that a more appropriate balance is struck between the absolutist tyranny of

theocracy and the intellectually dishonest and relativist position of secularism. The

reason for my feeling that such is necessary is that religion is far too important as a

factor in determining human interaction for the system to be indifferent to any and

all questions thereof.

With that, we now move on to discuss the current dilemma which

threatens representative democracy.

Section One: Introduction

Chapter Three: Corruptive Nature of Money in Politics

Chapter Three: Corruptive Nature of Money in Politics

Modern humanity has managed to survive and advance in large part thanks to our ever-changing approach to politics. Guiding and regulating the interaction of humans with one another, this characteristic of our species was one of the first – if not the first – major benefit of our ability to speak. This is because politics determines issues of distribution, justice, and development. It is the very foundation of civilized life.

Over the course of our evolution, politics has progressively changed to reflect the needs, concerns, and interests of the times. At times, though, this progress has been derailed by greed and a lust for power, thus leading to the emergence of tyrants and oligarchs. Presently, the American political system is in sincere danger of experiencing such a transition. This is due to the elevated role played by money in our politics. With such heavy reliance on the size of one's wallet, there is a legitimate reason to be concerned about certain aspects of the representative democracy we Americans enjoy.

For starters, there is issue advocacy. In the ideal society, all sides would start the debate on an equal footing, with the winning side prevailing based on the support of its expressed position. Sadly, this is not the case in a political system which is predominantly based on information distributed by a private media market. As a result, getting the word out for a position more often than not requires all interested parties to have the means to pay for such. The hints of direct democracy present in America – such as the initiative, the popular referendum, and the recall - are limited by this need for money to spend on the effort. Though there have been exceptions, the side which raises and spends the most money during the campaign tends to have the best shot at securing a victory.

Likewise, this constant requirement to have a hefty "war chest", as the pundits call it, produces an atmosphere wherein the campaigning never ends as candidates for office are always on the lookout for donors. This leads to the fundraising events which distract officeholders from doing the job they were elected to do all in the name of telling wealthy supporters everything they want to hear before their pocketbooks are opened. From time to time, desperation on the part of candidates and prospective donors generates the kind of quid pro quo governance which corrupts the system in the end. What's troubling is that this problem will only be exacerbated as the limits on campaign contributions continue to be eroded.

In the "[e]xecutive [s]ummary" of their report, Anthony Corrado (Corrado, Anthony et al, 2010) and other coauthors writing for the Brookings Institute prefaced their position on contribution limits by noting that "limits [have] limits" (para. 2). Though it may be a tough pill to swallow, this critique about limits is painfully true. Yes, it is ideal to cap the amount that one can contribute to a campaign, but in a society with multiple avenues for free expression the ability to restrict an individual's political expenditures becomes increasingly difficult. At what point does it become obvious that private donations are the root of the problem?

In many ways, the Citizens United decision grossly exacerbated already-existing problems with the system overall. Compared to the Watergate era – as one

Richard Hasen noted (Hasen, Richard L., 2012) – the campaign atmosphere in the

post-Citizens United era has made Richard Nixon's political crimes seem petty.

For instance, the once-scandalous contribution of a few million dollars to a

presidential candidate now would be preferable to the current unlimited ability to

contribute to a so-called Super PAC which need only worry about "coordinating"

with a candidate (paras. 1, 3-4). Today – as can also be seen in Hasen's article -,

influence bought indirectly is more poignant than it ever was when done directly

(para. 7).

  With respect to how money impacts running for office, Congress is

increasingly becoming an exclusive club that hardly represents the people. The

reason is that the cost of campaigning continues to increase at an alarming rate.

For instance, consider the fact that – as reported in a *New York Daily News* article

in 2013 (Knowles, David, 2013) – the 2012 election saw the average "price of

winning" in the Senate jump to over ten million dollars – which means that

candidates must raise about $14,000 per day of the campaign – and House seats

themselves cost approximately 1.7 million dollars to secure. Just as the author

highlighted, this produces an atmosphere wherein fundraising – not governing –

becomes the elected official's job (paras. 3-6).

  What's equally disturbing is that the cost of running for Congress is just

one small pixel of the bigger picture. The Sunlight Foundation pointed out in

January 2013 (Harper, Jake, 2013) that the 2012 election – thanks to the Citizens

United decision – was the costliest election in history at "more than [seven] billion

[dollars]" (paras. 1-2)! At this rate, what is to stop the cost of elections from rising

to a trillion dollars within a generation? In time, it will be virtually impossible for

anyone who isn't rich and well-connected to ever consider any elective office.

That's right, I said "any".

Keeping the fundraising question in mind, it is also relevant to point out

how the right – and dare I say, duty - to dissent is significantly hindered by the

obstacle of money. Devoid of an equal playing field, the best-funded candidates

enjoy the promise of "safe seats", as they merely have to spend enough money

attacking the other candidate who may or may not be able to refute or otherwise

respond in kind. A well-financed incumbent has an even greater advantage since

the "war chest" only helps to prevent any potential challenger from attaining a

comparable name recognition status. All of this creates a weak representative

democracy, since the elected may be winning by default.

Of course, the system's corruption doesn't end with the election of a

candidate to office. Beyond the ballot box, the political process is further

influenced by way of lobbying for government action. In this respect, a polity such

as is found in the United States becomes further detached from the populace and

this is not a new problem. Again, the amount of money that an organization has

determines its clout.

Compounding this dilemma further is the troubling fact that lobbyists

have a knack for writing legislation for the elected. Take, for instance, the political

muscle of a lobbying organization known as ALEC. According to the *New York

Times* (McIntire, Mike, 2012), the American Legislative Exchange Council – an

organization with members representing corporate interests as well as a number of elected officials – possesses enough clout in government to successfully petition for legislative bills to be killed as well as to help draft bills affecting a number of policies ranging from guns to voting rights (paras. 2, 4-6). As the saying goes, "this is why we can't have nice things".

The standard counterargument to highlighting the glaring problem with the ostensibly-growing role of corporations in our politics is to point out that political action committees operated by unions enjoy a certain degree of power as well. Undoubtedly, this is true in a number of communities and regions, but it is laughable to suggest that unions provide a sufficient balance to those PACs ran by corporate and otherwise wealthy interests. There can be no denying that the wealthiest in society have a key advantage over all others seeking attention for their concerns. Even so, whether wealthy or not, the fact that lobbying for government action tends to be connected to promises and donations made during a campaign – past, present, or future – is a warning sign that the system is in danger of misuse and abuse.

The fundamental problem with a democracy dependent upon the flow of money is that it predetermines the winners and losers by creating a permanently powerful class and a permanently powerless class. Accessibility becomes more important than participation – an essential component of democracy - under such a design. In effect, the nature of this approach – if unaddressed - transforms the democracy into an oligarchy; or even a plutocracy. Ultimately, with money at the helm, greed conquers the purpose of society and shreds the social contract in favor of a more despotic or chaotic atmosphere wherein every man and woman is

compelled to fend for themselves at the expense of everyone else.

As long as a society – democratic or not – relies on purchased access it

can not be reasonably expected to serve and/or represent the citizenry. Nor is it

possible for peace and stability to remain under these conditions. Depriving any

one group within a society of their equal share of power incites resentment and

later produces revolution. Unless it is used by and for the public, money is the

most significant force behind same said deprivation. This is because money –

when spent privately – is an extension of one's personal interests, and those

interests are more often than not selfishly-aimed.

Yet another concern is the issue of keeping the powerful honest. In lieu of

an even playing field without the obstacle of money, there is little incentive for

transparency. For this reason, back room deals and quid pro quo policymaking

become commonplace as the few wield their influence either to spite the many or

simply to further expand their wealth. Therein lays the path to secretive and -

eventually - oppressive governance.

Why is this so crucial? Because transparency allows the people to know

what is being done in their name. Transparency safeguards the populace from

tyranny in all forms and is typically enhanced with public hearings as well as the

right to a free press. Most importantly, if there is no transparency, then there is no

accountability.

With respect to accountability, there can be none unless a powerful entity

feels that its actions have consequences. Holding others accountable is the power to limit the abuse and misuse of their duties while incentivizing their good

performance. However, a political system which favors the fortunate minority's

input produces a political culture with officials pledging – via their actions – fealty

to the same. In America, the shift of influence towards the few has been obvious

with one column in the *New York Times* (Lessig, Lawrence, 2011) pointing out

that "[l]ess than [one] percent of Americans [exceed $200 in donating to

campaigns]", and that an even smaller number of people max-out (para. 6).

In the wake of Citizens United, - as was discussed by David Knowles

(Knowles, David, 2013) – members of Congress are now almost entirely beholden

to corporate interests for fear that the wrong vote will earn them a flurry of attack

ads thereby (paras. 8-9). That is the very definition of accountability, but the

wrong type. Obviously, as individual citizens, corporate employees from the top to

the bottom of the totem pole have a right to expect their voices to be heard and

their democratic wrath to be feared. Again, the issue is whether their voices and

wrath are disproportionately more important than everyone else's.

In writing the Citizens United opinion – as reported by NPR (Tedford,

Deborah, 2010) – Justice Kennedy said that "[t]he court has recognized…First

Amendment protection [as extending] to corporations" (para. 24). Let that sink in

for a moment. Corporations, an entity created by humans, has now been granted

the same rights within the First Amendment to the United States Constitution as

are afforded to living, breathing, humans. Clearly, this paves the way for a new set

of constitutional crises in the years to come. That is, unless the American people take it upon themselves to demand an end to this trend which has allowed for the rise of America's very own oligarchy.

There are two major reasons why I've highlighted America's money-in-politics crisis. For starters, it is the political culture with which I'm most familiar. Secondly, many political and historical experts recognize the American political system as being the world's most important. Not only because this country is currently the sole superpower, but because ours is the most advanced of the world's democracies. So, it is absolutely imperative that the American people reclaim the reigns of power here at home before the rest of the world can be expected to rise up in favor of democracy.

Taming the political money beast is a must for anyone of any political stripe. No matter your personal views, the issue of rescuing the democracy on this front can not be avoided. Reason being, that the powerful will never be inclined to care about any ideas or issues beyond those held in high esteem by the interests paying the political bills. In essence, as long as money dictates the course taken the complaints of the powerless will continue to be tantamount to the buzzing of an irritating insect. Change can not happen otherwise, not even the change to be discussed in the chapters to follow.

References:

McIntire, M. (2012, April 21). Conservative Nonprofit Acts as a Stealth Business

Lobbyist. *The New York Times on the Web*. Retrieved November 18,

2013, from:

http://www.nytimes.com/2012/04/22/us/alec-a-tax-exempt-group-mixes-

legislators-and-lobbyists.html?pagewanted=all&_r=0

Corrado, A., Malbin, M.J., Mann, T.E., & Ornstein, N.J. (2010). Reform in an age

of

networked campaigns: how to foster citizen participation through small

donors

and volunteers. Brookings Institute website. Retrieved November 18,

2013, from:

http://www.brookings.edu/research/reports/2010/01/14-campaign-

finance-reform

Harper, J. (2013, January 31). Total 2012 election spending: $7 billion. Sunlight

Foundation website. Retrieved November 27, 2013, from:

http://reporting.sunlightfoundation.com/2013/total-2012-election-

spending-7-billion/

Hasen, R.L. (2012, July 19). Worse Than Watergate: The new campaign finance

order

puts the corruption of the 1970s to shame. *Slate on the web*. Retrieved

November

20, 2013, from:

http://www.slate.com/articles/news_and_politics/jurisprudence/2012/07/c

ampaign_finance_after_citizens_united_is_worse_than_watergate_.html

Knowles, D. (2013, March 11). U.S. Senate seat now costs $10.5 million to win,

on

average, while US House seat costs, $1.7 million, new analysis of FEC

data

shows. *New York Daily News on the web.* Retrieved November 26, 2013,

from:

http://www.nydailynews.com/news/politics/cost-u-s-senate-seat-10-5-

million-article-1.1285491

Lessig, L. (2011, November 16). More Money Can Beat Big Money. *The New*

York

Times on the web. Retrieved November 26, 2013, from:

http://www.nytimes.com/2011/11/17/opinion/in-campaign-financing-

more-money-can-beat-big-money.html?_r=0

Tedford, D. (2010, January 21). Supreme Court Rips Up Campaign Finance Laws.

NPR

on the web. Retrieved November 27, 2013, from:

http://www.npr.org/templates/story/story.php?storyId=122805666

Section Two: Justice and Security

Chapter Four: International Protection

Chapter Four: International Protection

Among the most important features of civilization is the need to promote

order and justice. In a world which finds itself "shrinking" more and more with

every passing generation, it must be resolved that a framework for international

justice be established. There are presently a great number of matters which are

dealt with by international organizations such as the European Union and the

United Nations. However, the weak standards of cooperation leave much of the

work unfinished, thereby passing the buck to lower levels of governance which

may be ill-equipped to address such. So, it is incumbent upon us to mold a

stronger, more collective approach which recognizes the responsibility of all the

world's states to uphold the rule of law.

The need to distinguish international law and the enforcement thereof

from the same on the national and local levels – both of which will be discussed

later within this section – stems from the differing nature of these crimes.

International crimes are violations of standards agreed upon by all of humanity.

What this means is that the international crime is an affront to every person, and

should be prosecuted on the global stage by a global justice system. At this point,

it helps to highlight some of the more obvious examples of the very offenses

which require the international community's response.

For starters, there are the varying levels of piracy. Far from the humorous

and slightly lovable image as portrayed by Hollywood movies and family theme

parks, this criminal element has wreaked havoc on the global exchange of goods

for several centuries. An abstract of Lawrence Azubuike's 2009 article on piracy

(Azubuike, Lawrence, 2009) – as shared by the Golden Gate University website –

notes that pirates were once perceived to be "enemies of human kind", but were difficult to tame since a number of countries were tolerant and often in league therewith. Now, this threat to economic stability has been making a comeback and demands a modernized approach (para. 1).

Another crime which requires international cooperation is human trafficking. Tragically, the vast majority of victims are not fortunate enough to have a Liam Neeson-type figure come to the rescue. Instead, real life is far more frightening, and the danger of being kidnapped and sold into perpetual sexual slavery exists for men and women all around the world. Clearly, it is not enough for humanity to leave this highly-organized operation to local or even regional police efforts. Reason being, that the ability of these criminals to evade justice and to spirit away their "product" remains superior to any efforts at swift containment within a set jurisdiction. To put it another way, this crime is one which demands a global jurisdiction.

Then, there is the unavoidable issue of terrorism. Yes, this is a criminal act which exists in varying degrees and can be an international threat, a regional one, or even just limited to a local jurisdiction. Sometimes, the word "terrorism" is so loosely defined that each society could consider almost any action which dissents from the respective government as such. For that reason, local, national, and regional governments should be permitted to police the "terrorism" that they perceive as a threat to their way of life; so long as human rights are respected in the process. Internationally, though, there is a desperate need for a change of course in how this matter is handled.

In the history of civilization, international law has been established via treaties. One major flaw with this approach is that the enforcement of a treaty is typically the threat of sanction or military action. Then again, many treaties are easily violated because signatories reserve the inherent right to withdraw at any time; though, not without diplomatic consequences, at the very least. Moreover, the threat of punitive action by a treaty's governing body – if such exists – is often weakened by a hesitance to follow through for fear of creating or exacerbating an international crisis.

Take, for instance, the handling of piracy. Of course, not all pirates commit their acts via ships and boats. International law – as the Motion Picture Association of America tells us ("Protecting Creativity Around The World", n.d.) – also guards against the pirating of "intellectual property". This is currently done by way of trade agreements and commits the signatories to ensure that their respective laws will respect the copyrights of foreign property owners (paras. 1-3). Yet, the piracy of movies and other forms of entertainment remain rampant especially as far as the so-called Third World is concerned. Perhaps it is because of the lax resources available to enforce standards set on the global stage.

Lindsey King's article found at the University of Denver's website highlights (King, Lindsey, 2009) the importance of a great number of treaties in combating human trafficking. Again, this is problematic in its current form given the fact that participating states must be willing to uphold their end of the deal (pg. 88). King points out that many feel a "regional solution" works best in dealing with transnational crimes (pg. 89). Then again, it is likewise noted that enforcing international law often runs into a number of problems such as limited resources and legal knowledge in addition to communication barriers for the trafficking victims unfortunate enough to wind up in a different country (pp. 89-90). All in all, while treaties have helped to maintain some semblance of order, they are primarily only good for establishing a foundation of trade terms and at bringing an end to hostilities between warring parties.

Part of the weakness of international law enforcement by way of treaties is that extradition is not universally practiced. Professional criminals are usually quite informed as to which countries do not extradite, or to whom they don't. What this creates is a dilemma of injustice wherein crimes result in no punishment simply because the perpetrators were either clever or well-connected enough to beat the authorities across the right border. Without addressing this, justice will remain a dream for countless victims around the world.

At the moment, the failure of treaty-based international law to maintain order has produced an incentive for some to use their militaries to exact justice. Naturally, this causes more trouble than it sets out to resolve, and for the same reason that Gandhi lamented how "an eye for an eye" results in a blind world. The reason for this is that the tools of justice and war are geared towards different objectives; with the latter looking to conquer an enemy and the former attempting to maintain and uphold the rule of law on behalf of the collective. Eventually, with a number of world powers taking the law into their own hands, the rule of law begins to break down.

There is no greater – nor more ironically tragic - example of a world power wreaking such havoc on law and order for the sake of revenge than the rule of law's foremost advocate: the United States in the aftermath of September 11th, 2001. In the introductory pages of a report to Congress on George W. Bush's antiterrorism policies pertinent to justice, it was mentioned (Elsea, Jennifer, 2001) that the administration's belief in the need for extralegal military tribunals and detainment at sites like Guantanamo Bay was fueled by a then-prevalent fear that a public trial would become a "circus" or result in the release of suspected terrorists. Additionally, there was the redefinition of these terrorists as "enemy combatants". Regarding the enemy combatant designation, those categorized as such were seen as falling in between "prisoners of war" and traditional "criminals". Therefore, terrorists were to be dealt with differently than both of those categories (pp. 1-2).

If even the supposed standard-bearer of modern civilization is not immune to the temptation of vigilante justice in a world with weak laws and weaker enforcement mechanisms, then the time has long since passed for reform. In order to end the legal chaos and establish order, a new global federalism must be adopted. Using the United Nations to facilitate the discussion and transition, the people of the world must compel their respective governments to help draft and then ratify a constitution not unlike the American Constitution. As a part of this new superfederalist design, there ought to be a framework for combating international crimes.

Since terrorism is the most controversial crime, it receives the most attention here. That's because combating crimes such as intellectual property theft and human trafficking don't produce the type of policy debates seen with

terrorism. As mentioned before, international terrorism is currently seen as a

military problem. Simply put, this has to change.

Maria Alvanou of the Research Institute for European and American

Studies made mention (Alvanou, Maria, n.d.) of an important dilemma created by

treating criminal acts such as terrorism as an act warranting military retaliation or

a war-based mindset. Basically, declaring war on any act legitimizes and

politicizes such. By dealing with criminals like terrorists via the justice system, the

act in question is rendered taboo and is deprived of any reasonable – or arguably

civilized - badge of honor to be used in recruitment propaganda (paras. 3-4). Just

as Alvanou believes, it must be said that the military can serve some role in

dealing with international crime (para. 9). Though, same said role would have to

be limited to assisting in some international policing effort as hosted by the

world's collective states in order to enforce international laws and prosecute the

violators thereof.

Ben Saul – in writing for the European Society of International Law

(Saul, Ben, n.d.) – points out that the push for internationally criminalizing

terrorism would help to distinguish such acts from other international crimes.

Moreover, the precedent for setting an international standard can be found in the

Nuremburg Principles wherein a crime is considered to be of international concern

when it is "grave" and when it can no longer "be left within the exclusive

jurisdiction of the State" (pg. 1). Whenever terrorist acts cross borders and/or

threaten the world's stability, it can likewise be seen as a matter for the international community (pg. 2). Ultimately, developing a universal definition of criminal terrorism at the international level can assist in bringing these criminals to justice with protections for nation-states against terrorists masquerading as refugees and by improving extradition – in lieu of prosecution – policies (pp. 12-13).

Fortunately, there readily exists a fledgling institution which can be employed to usher in these essential changes; the International Criminal Court. By including this court in a new global constitution, there will no longer be a need for the failed treaties. Crimes committed on a global – or a transnational – scale will finally have a civilized remedy. As Ken Gude points out (Gude, Ken, 2010), the criminal court has a far better and reliable record in holding suspects accountable than the approach which attempts to avoid their status as criminals (para. 16). It is time to modernize and civilize international justice. Now, we look at matters pertaining to national protection.

References:

Alvanou, M. (n.d.). Terrorists and Justice: Thinking of Legal Problems Due to the

Military Approach of Counterterrorism. Research Institute for European

and

American Studies website. Retrieved January 2, 2014, from:

http://www.rieas.gr/research-areas/greek-studies/255.html

Azubuike, L. (2009). International Law Regime Against Piracy. Golden Gate

University

website. Retrieved December 29, 2013, from:

http://digitalcommons.law.ggu.edu/annlsurvey/vol15/iss1/4/

Elsea, J. (2001, December 11). Terrorism and the Law of War: Trying Terrorists

as War

Criminals before Military Commissions. *CRS Report for Congress*.

Retrieved

December 24, 2013, from:

http://fpc.state.gov/documents/organization/7951.pdf

Gude, K. (2010, January 20). Criminal Courts Are Tougher on Terrorists than

Military

Detention. Center for American Progress website. Retrieved December

20, 2013,

from:

http://www.americanprogress.org/issues/security/news/2010/01/20/7207/

criminal-courts-are-tougher-on-terrorists-than-military-detention/

King, L. (2009). International law and human trafficking. *Human Rights & Human*

Welfare, Topical Research Digest: Human Rights and Human

Trafficking, 88-103. University of Denver website. Retrieved January 6,

2014, from:

http://www.du.edu/korbel/hrhw/researchdigest/trafficking/InternationalLa

w.pdf

Protecting Creativity Around The World. (n.d.). Motion Picture Association of

America

website. Retrieved January 1, 2014, from:

http://www.mpaa.org/contentprotection/copyright-laws/international

Saul, B. (n.d.) Three Reasons for Defining and Criminalizing Terrorism. European

Society of International Law website. Retrieved December 25, 2013,

from:

http://www.esil-sedi.eu/sites/default/files/Saul_0.PDF

Section Two: Justice and Security

Chapter Five: National Protection

Chapter Five: National Protection

The definition of a "nation" is a question subject to much debate. So as to avoid any confusion here, references to "nations" should be understood as references to "nation-states", such as the United States of America. With that clarification out of the way, let us proceed.

Protecting the nation is as important from a domestic policy perspective as it is from the foreign policy viewpoint. Sometimes, the threat can be purely economic, and initially not seem so dire. Other times, the nation's stability could be in danger via a well-coordinated insurrection. In between are crimes that may or may not be violent and potentially destabilizing, yet still demand a broad response. When threats to security and justice are too broad for the locale, yet still confined within a nation's borders, it is incumbent upon the national collective to act.

If one were to measure the severity of a national threat based on the level of violence or physical harm involved, we would find crimes against the people's economy at the very bottom. This is not to say that these crimes are less concerning or harmful, but that they are "bloodless". In a way, economic crimes rival crimes against the people's state as far as the risk of creating chaos is concerned. It all depends on the consequences for inaction on the offense at issue. For example, the economic crimes of illegal insider trading and antitrust violations – both of which will be discussed more soon – may share a common national scope, but they are not equally threatening to the stability of the nation's economy; since the risk of monopoly outweighs the risk of what may be an unfair trading advantage. Make no mistake about it, if an economy becomes overly corrupt and/or imbalanced, the "bloodless" can soon trigger bloodshed.

One notch up on the scale of severity is the crime against the people's environment. Environmental offenses are slightly more physically harmful than economic crimes because of the direct and indirect affects that such can have on the public health. It is in the national interest to be good environmental stewards, as the U.S. Department of Justice website points out ("Prosecution of Federal Pollution Crimes", 2013). Laws aimed at preventing the intentional poisoning of Mother Earth – which mostly occurs in an attempt to satisfy one's greed (paras. 2-3) - must be initially enforced as a nationally collective effort, since the long-term consequences thereof are difficult to contain in an isolated region. Like with economics, unabated abuse of the environment can produce an unstable political atmosphere which can result in societal unrest. So, neither threat – despite their positioning at the lower end of the threat scale – should be underestimated.

Next, the people's safety comes to mind. As a wide-ranging category of crimes, there are many offenses which qualify even at the national level. There is even a place for laws pertaining to kidnapping at this level. At FindLaw's website ("Kidnapping", n.d. para. 1), you see that U.S. federal law currently reinforces state laws which protect against the forced movement of people from one location to the next. This type of overlap in law can be nationally useful if the crime here – as is the case with all national crimes – extends beyond an individual region's scope.

Obviously, there is another qualifying group of crimes against the people's safety. An article in the *Huffington Post* covered (Lohr, David, 2013) a number of the "most notorious criminals" to ever captivate the American people.

Among them were the serial murderers Ted Kaczynski and Ted Bundy (paras. 6,

11). Serial criminals like them, whose offenses spanned large sections of the

country, require a national response. Reason being, that they pose a threat to the

nation as a whole.

At the very top of the scale are the crimes perpetrated against the people's

state. Since these acts run the risk of violently toppling an entire system, they

deserve the most vigilant attention. By visiting the Cornell University Law

School's Legal Information Institute website ("18 U.S. Code Chapter 115 –

TREASON, SEDITION, AND SUBVERSIVE ACTIVITIES", n.d.), you can see

the section of U.S. law reserved for the ultimate national criminals: traitors.

Treasonous, seditious, and otherwise rebellious crimes undermine the legitimacy

of a government, and when such is committed against any form of democracy it is

an affront to the people represented thereby and to democracies all around the

world. In other words, crimes against the people's state must be deterred in order

to uphold the legitimacy of both the specific government in question as well as the

form of governance itself.

To shield against threats to the people's safety and state, the best

contemporary approach is a national police force. For an easily-recognizable

example, America's national police force – the Federal Bureau of Investigation –

began out of the Progressive Era, as seen in the "Brief History" page at the

agency's website ("A Brief History of the FBI", n.d). With President Theodore

Roosevelt and his like-minded Attorney General, Charles Bonaparte, the seeds for

what would later become the "Bureau" were planted via "a force of special agents" in accordance with the Progressive principles of expertise – not politics –

determining said appointments. Despite this country's initial opposition to "big"

government, the era's mood and the "shrinking" nature of our culture and

interaction led many to support a greater role for federal intervention so as to

ensure justice (paras. 1-4); a role which the FBI would eventually prove capable of

fulfilling as far as national protection was concerned.

Defending the people's environment isn't a cakewalk itself, either. Since

the long-term effects – including the question of how widespread the damage will

ultimately be - of criminal pollution can be complicated to estimate, no local or

individual regional government can or should be expected to keep such crimes in

check alone. That is why the nation as a whole – and even the larger global

community, if the situation is severe enough – must work as one to maintain our

green plants, clear skies, and blue waters. The modern American approach to this

responsibility is found in the Environmental Protection Agency which acts to

defend America's portion of dear old Mother Earth by enforcing our rather

lackluster – by western world standards – environmental regulations with the

threat of "heavy" fines for those looking to hurt the planet more than what is

"permissible". Tragically, despite the good intentions of this agency, its meager

budget, limited power, and inability to adequately challenge the powerful

economic interests who do the most harm render it inept as a protector.

With regards to the people's economy, protection is about preserving a

proper – or fair - balance in the distribution of the nation's wealth. For example, in

order to safeguard "the fairness and integrity of the securities markets", the

Securities and Exchange Commission polices ("Insider Trading", 2013) what's

called "insider trading" to ensure that the only such trading going on is what has

been authorized both by law and the commission itself (paras. 1, 2, & 4). Devoid

of this policing, the stock market would be rife with underhanded tactics in

business dealings just to make a quick buck no matter who gets hurt. It isn't that

such doesn't exist now, but it would be far worse in that major corporate decisions

could be driven by one's desire to boost his or her own personal fortunes in the

betting game that is the stock exchange. To put it another way, it would be akin to

letting a ball player place a bet on a game that he or she planned to intentionally

lose; or somehow cheat to win.

Just as is the case with all the other national crimes, there are varying

degrees of severity in economic offenses. The Federal Trade Commission's

website ("The Antitrust Laws", n.d.) highlights one of the most important aspects

of national protection: antitrust laws. Here, the consumer is shielded from the

worst produced by monopolies. By preventing "unlawful mergers" – which are

designated as such when there is a failure to secure authorization ahead of time in

the event that the merging entities are large enough to have a significant impact on

the market (para. 7) -, government agencies like the FTC are helping to maintain

reasonable prices and an arguably better quality in our services (paras. 1-2). It is

vital to prevent the emergence of large market monopolies both for the consumer

and for the economy's health as a whole, since the real danger here is economic

tyranny by way of the concentration of too much wealth and power into fewer

hands.

In looking towards the future in protecting the nation, we must recognize the strengths and weaknesses of the current way we do so. At the moment, there is far too much conflict and confusion as to where the local and national jurisdictions begin and end. Some overlap is fine, but an excessive amount can hinder justice rather than promoting such. For that reason, clear distinctions of the boundaries between these levels of governance – as well as where cooperation is essential – must be defined and strictly obeyed. Again, federalism is the only structure of government which can both effectively maintain national order and respect the semi-autonomy of each governing level.

Now, to conclude this section, we move to discussing the matter of local protection.

References:

18 U.S. Code Chapter 115 – TREASON, SEDITION, AND SUBVERSIVE

ACTIVITIES. (n.d.). Cornell University Law School. Legal Information

Institute

Website. Retrieved February 21, 2014, from:

http://www.law.cornell.edu/uscode/text/18/part-I/chapter-115

A Brief History of the FBI. (n.d.). The Federal Bureau of Investigation Website.

Retrieved February 25, 2014, from: http://www.fbi.gov/about-

us/history/brief-history/brief-history

The Antitrust Laws. (n.d.). The Federal Trade Commission Website. Retrieved

February

26, 2014, from: http://www.ftc.gov/tips-advice/competition-

guidance/guide-antitrust-laws/antitrust-laws

Insider Trading. (2013, January 15). The U.S. Securities and Exchange

Commission

Website. Retrieved February 27, 2014, from:

https://www.sec.gov/answers/insider.htm

Kidnapping. (n.d.). FindLaw Website. Retrieved February 28, 2014, from:

http://criminal.findlaw.com/criminal-charges/kidnapping.html

Lohr, D. (2013, September 12). 10 Most Notorious Criminals In American

History. *The*

Huffington Post on the Web. Retrieved March 2, 2014, from:

http://www.huffingtonpost.com/2013/09/12/americas-most-notorious-

criminals_n_3761487.html?utm_hp_ref=serial-killers

Prosecution of Federal Pollution Crimes. (2013, September). The United States

Department of Justice website. Retrieved March 4, 2014, from:

http://www.justice.gov/enrd/5471.htm

The Pillars of Unitism
63

Section Two: Justice and Security

Chapter Six: Local Protection

Chapter Six: Local Protection

Regardless of how important crimes on an international, national, or subnational level may be, individual citizens tend to see such as being too abstract to care about. For them, local offenses against the public matter the most, as it affects their sense of security at home. In this respect, gang violence, home invasion, rape, and murder are perceived as being among a collective's gravest threats since the danger is immediate and can't be seen as abstract. Here, the remedy must be developed by the community and in the interest of everyone – not excluding the unsavory characters - within. More specifically, deterring local crime ought to focus more on rehabilitating those who've committed minor offenses whilst harshly punishing the most violent offenders.

First and foremost, it helps to understand what drives our fellow citizens to defy the law to begin with. These people aren't born with the desire to commit crimes of any sort. Instead, the lack of appreciation for law and order is nurtured via a combination of factors with life experience and one's "environment" – more socially, than naturally, speaking in this context – being chief among them. A society can not hope to adequately curb criminal behavior if it does not first attempt to understand the motivation and background thereof.

Economics plays a crucial part in many societal twists and turns, and its influence in local crime can't be brushed aside. The economic theory of crime – as seen in a brief by the New Zealand Ministry of Justice ("Theories of the Causes of Crime", 2009) – suggests that crime is committed in response to a cost-benefit analysis of the economic pros and cons of such acts. Here, the solution is believed to be found in making improvements as far as "educational [and/] or job opportunities" are concerned (pg. 4). In other words, give people hope, and they will be less inclined to spread fear.

Beyond the issue of providing hope to the hopeless is combating boredom; particularly among society's outcasts. The popular idiom which says that "idle hands are the Devil's playground" holds some truth to it in that a lack of constructive activities for people – especially the young and impressionable – can be a recipe for destructive behavior. Criminal activity – the *Encyclopedia of Crime and Justice* tells us (Witt, Robert, & Witte, Ann D., 2000) – is akin to a sport for young men, with a high rate of participation for the socially excluded by the time one reaches his thirties. Yet again, it is suggested – by the article's authors – that educational, and job-creating, programs receive increased investment so as to curb the negative impact produced by same said exclusion (pp. 2-3).

Then again, exclusion from society is meaningless if the community involved isn't united. Aric Hall (Hall, Aric, 2007) notes that many crimes can be traced back to "social disorganization", and that "[social ecology studies] indicate that ecological conditions predispose individuals to crime". Such conditions include the afore-referenced local – or personal – economic reality, a troublesome family life, as well as a broken sense of community (pg. 4). How can community members be expected to respect their neighbors in such an adversarial atmosphere?

While considering this thought that a "disorganized" – or even a poorly organized - community is partially to blame for the crime rate being higher in some locales as opposed to others, it seems logical to propose that more be done to encourage citizens to reach out and work with their neighbors. Moreover, the role

of policing is seemingly made easier when there is enhanced cooperation between

community members and those walking the beat. Even in our increasingly-

interconnected world, protecting the public's safety is reliant on the willful

communication of a community's needs and concerns to law enforcement

interests. In lieu of such, the only real alternative – aside of permitting chaos – is

the establishment of an oppressive police state; an option which is not conducive

for a flourishing democracy.

Instead of having a detached and sometimes seemingly-oppressive police

force, one approach – as highlighted by the Bureau of Justice Statistics website

("Community Policing", n.d.) – looks to bring the community and their officers

together in a constructive partnership known as "community policing". In said

partnership, the officers make themselves available to members and groups of the

community, offer educational assistance, devise strategies with the locals, lend a

helping hand to those in need, and patrol the area by "foot and bicycle" as opposed

to the less intimate use of vehicular transportation (para. 1). By creating such a

union between law enforcement and the community, the men and women charged

with "protecting and serving" the neighborhood become more like active

neighbors than some "foreign" occupying force. As a result, the people benefiting

from as much develop a greater sense of trust and are more likely to do their civic

duty in helping the police maintain local security.

Unfortunately, fighting crime isn't as simple as dispatching uniformed

men and women to troubled neighborhoods. What hinders far too many cities across the world is that policing is an expensive investment. On the other hand, when local resources are inadequate to support community policing, upper levels of government can be of some assistance. For instance, the U.S. Department of Justice – via its COPS program, according to the website for said program ("About", n.d., para. 1) – helps to promote such by way of "sharing information and making grants to [local] police departments". If left purely to their own devices, many communities would be rendered inept at dealing with crime since there are no two communities with the same resources available to them. For that reason, there must be cooperation at all levels of government to tame criminal activity.

Realistically, the people can't solely depend on the government spending money to promote community policing. To an extent, the responsibility to ensure security in a truly free society rests on the citizens' shoulders. This brings us back to the issue of getting people involved with their neighborhood, as the ancient notion of being your "brother's keeper" remains relevant today. Participation isn't just essential to make democracy work, but also to protect the rights and interests of all free men beyond the ballot box.

In order to stimulate participation as well as to help with community policing, neighborhood watches have proven to be quite the effective tool. USAonwatch.org discusses ("About Neighborhood Watch", n.d.) the role of these watches as using "education and common sense" to assist the police in doing their job. Moreover, it is stressed that only the police should "take action" – meaning, no vigilante justice -, given that there is too much risk with citizens taking the law into their own hands (paras. 1-2). The basic spirit of the watch was once conveyed by someone named Rosenbaum, when he remarked that "if social disorganization is the problem and if traditional agents of social control no longer are performing adequately, we need to find alternative ways to strengthen informal social control and to restore a 'sense of neighborhood'" (para. 4). Basically, the key to local protection is unity.

What about the men and women who choose to violate the law? The contemporary approach is to send local criminals to a jail until a sentence can be determined or for a short-term stay as punishment for a so-called "nonviolent crime". By "nonviolent crime", it is obvious that much of what such entails is illegal drug use. Though a number of communities in the civilized world have "decriminalized" certain drugs – as well as legalizing the recreational use thereof in a few instances -, the war on drugs continues to serve as a shackle inhibiting the progress of struggling impoverished citizens across the planet.

In many ways, current local jailing practices merely countenance the abusive cycle of crime and poverty. The Bureau of Justice Statistics website tells us ("Local jail inmates and jail facilities", n.d. para. 1) that the local jails serve one of two functions: a temporary holding place for prisoners, suspects, and even the mentally ill, as well as the imprisonment of local offenders for crimes warranting less than a year "behind bars". No wonder the prison population is so bloated. Yes, there are crimes which absolutely must warrant a punishment which separates the offender from society, but it is time to reconsider the terms of what commands an extended stay beyond the judge's decree.

The archaic prohibition of harmless, yet unsavory, behavior ranging from recreational marijuana use to prostitution ought to be lifted so as to permit the prosecution of far more legitimate crimes. With legalization comes the ability to regulate and tax; so that safety can be insured, the black market can be undercut, and so the public as a whole can share in the generated revenue. In theory, this would significantly reduce the threats of laced drugs, human trafficking, and organized crime – given that such is largely financed by way of these black market-based sales -, which would assist in dealing with such problems on the national and international levels. Also, the potential for job creation and boosted economic growth is undeniable.

In combating crime, neighborhood watching should be an activity promoted – possibly even mandated, as determined by the locals - everywhere with revolving responsibilities so as to avoid any one citizen or group of citizens from either getting too stigmatized or too comfortable with the power to endanger others' liberties. As for community policing, so long as it remains necessary to have a police force, each officer should be required to familiarize his or herself with each member of the neighborhood to which they are assigned. Furthermore, it may be best for officers to actually be members of the neighborhoods they patrol. Eventually, the revolving neighborhood watch responsibilities could be accompanied by a revolving policing responsibility – which should constantly shift for the same reason as "watching" should - ; though, the "watch" and the "police" should never be shared by the same person or household at any given time.

Finally, the prosecution of criminals must be conducted in a more civilized way. Rehabilitating offenders so that they can rejoin the community as productive citizens needs to be the aim, unless the crime at issue is so offensive that it warrants a deterring punishment. In the case of those crimes so heinous that the perpetrator thereof is incorrigible, a permanent, quasi-isolated detention defined by a life of hard labor is the only option. This is preferable over the death penalty since many of these offenders have very little value of their own life to begin with and would welcome the prospect of execution with open arms. The goal is to deny them a state-sanctioned reward – such as an early sought-after death - for their behavior. Moreover, the labor could prove useful on an as-needed basis.

Regarding the criminals who are capable of rehabilitation, they must be given an adequate opportunity to assert themselves as responsible community members. First and foremost, the detention of these individuals should only be temporary as they await sentencing – which should not involve anything beyond limited house arrest and a probationary period with mandatory education and job training -, and it should be required that these citizens in rehab actively seek out work during and after their training. Additionally, the probation should only be permitted to end when it has been demonstrated that the citizen can maintain his or her employment – without any major issues - for more than a year. From there, the citizen could be seen as a reformed member of society.

Life, of course, is far more complex than this set of proposals suggests. An alarming number of criminals suffer from unattended mental illnesses – which will be discussed later in this book -, and some act out of pure boredom – another

matter requiring further discussion -, but the complicated nature of crime and

insecurity should not inhibit the contemplation of solutions. Humanity has made

amazing progress in advancing our production, in developing society, and in

dealing with law and order. We can not allow ourselves to be discouraged by the

lingering challenges posed by the worst of our nature. Instead, we must push

forward in uniting our purpose and making "peace on Earth" a reality. For now,

let's move on to yet another area where humanity has significantly progressed:

science.

References:

About. (n.d.). Community Oriented Policing Services, United States Department
of

       Justice website. Retrieved March 29, 2014, from:

       http://www.cops.usdoj.gov/Default.asp?Item=35

About Neighborhood Watch. (n.d.). USAonwatch.org website. Retrieved March
30,

       2014, from: http://www.usaonwatch.org/about/neighborhoodwatch.aspx?

Community Policing. (n.d.). Bureau of Justice Statistics website. Retrieved March
25,

       2014, from: http://www.bjs.gov/index.cfm?ty=tp&tid=81

Hall, A. (2007). Socio-economic theories of crime. Arichall.com website.
Retrieved

       March 31, 2014, from: http://www.arichall.com/academic/papers/hs8373-

       paper.pdf

Local jail inmates and jail facilities. (n.d.). Bureau of Justice Statistics website.
Retrieved

       March 28, 2014, from: http://www.bjs.gov/index.cfm?ty=tp&tid=12

Theories of the Causes of Crime. (2009, March). *Strategic Policy Brief*. New
Zealand

       Ministry of Justice. Retrieved April 1, 2014, from:

http://www.justice.govt.nz/justice-sector/drivers-of-crime/publications-and-background-information/documents/spb-theories-on-the-causes-of-crime

Witt, R., & Witte, A.D. (2000, July 19). Crime causation: economic theories. *Encyclopedia of Crime and Justice*, forthcoming 2001. Retrieved April 3, 2014, from:

http://wwwcache.surrey.ac.uk/economics/files/apaperspdf/ECON%2003-00.pdf

Section Three: Science

Chapter Seven: Environmentalism

Chapter Seven: Environmentalism

As hyperbolic as it sounds, humanity absolutely must come together to clean, protect, and preserve Mother Earth, or we are all going to die. Does that sound too alarmist? It shouldn't, because unless our species discovers another inhabitable planet that can be reached within a reasonable time, the apocalyptic prediction will be realized. Perhaps it is easier to make a comparison. Imagine that the Earth is an empty house with the windows left open, with a fireplace that is constantly burning, a fresh supply of food delivered every day, and a number of animals inhabiting it. Then, we move in and - over the course of a few days – start to alter some things by closing some of the windows, adding a few extra fireplaces, and consuming more and more food as time goes by.

Yes, this is a silly metaphor but consider for a second how the open windows represent important plants such as trees, and the fireplaces represent a greenhouse gas-producing action. Greenhouse gases have existed throughout the Earth's life, but it wasn't until humans discovered how to manipulate resources to boost our productivity that the output of these gases started to rise exponentially. Additionally, the removal of trees has gradually dismantled the Earth's natural counterbalance for the globe-warming gases. Taking into account what this seemingly ludicrous example has tried to convey, is it really so hyperbolic to claim that inaction with respect to the damage we're doing could mean extinction? Does it not seem more absurd to imply that our current course is sustainable?

It is likewise ridiculous to believe that humans are destroying the Earth itself. Truth be told, this planet has been around much longer than we have, and will outlast our species until the point when it is incinerated by our star. With that in mind, one must consider why it is that we often refer to this place as "Mother Earth". As will be discussed further in a later chapter, we humans – like all living things on this planet – came from the Earth's elements, and life has thrived because of a delicate balance which has largely existed since the first single-cell organisms started to appear. The instances wherein that balance was significantly disturbed produced the handful of mass extinction events that science has revealed to us. What this tells us is that Earth does not need us, but we and every other cohabitating living specimen depends on her and the maintenance of the aforementioned balance.

What's troubling is that humanity can't even come to a consensus about the things revealed to us by science. While many scientific fields are affected by this aversion to what our observational powers tell us, for now, the focus of this denialism will be on climate science's findings. In a world driven by the profit motive, the wealthiest interests hold the reins of power, and they are not fans of the type of science which suggests that their riches are derived from harmful activities. The logical response in their minds – so as to shield their bottom line – is to incite and promote doubt amongst the public about the science, thereby undermining any effort at building a consensus for action. Just as tobacco companies hired doctors to disseminate misinformation pertinent to the connection between their product and health problems, energy companies are presently in full force financing public ignorance about our warming and changing planet.

A world-renown Astrophysicist, Dr. Neil deGrasse-Tyson, once noted that, regardless of whether we accept it or not, the things that science tells us are true. This is ultimately what the industry's assault on science comes down to; we can not afford to keep debating the science when we should be *briefly* debating a solution. Education is essential to removing the shroud of confusion, but our time is precious and is wasting away with each passing day. At some point – if this nonsensical and distracting debate about the reliability of climate science isn't dispensed with -, humanity will be forced to choose between a comfortable and self-destructive living style and a drastic course correction. Bringing humanity to a consensus about this field of science is one of the few instances wherein it truly is a matter of life and death.

Realistically, the first objective must be to try and reach out to the people who refuse to acknowledge that we have a problem. Many of them are too reluctant to challenge their own conclusions and opinions, but it would be a mistake to assume that everyone within the denialist ranks is incorrigible. Still, the hurdles to guiding these potentially open-minded people must be addressed. Part of the problem in dealing with the changing climate is the level of confusion and misinformation as to what it all means. The State of Washington tried to tackle this hurdle head-on by clarifying ("What is climate change?", n.d.) what distinguishes climate from weather, noting that the climate of a region – or the planet overall – "is the average weather [as measured] over a long time period". Moreover, the difference between climate change and global warming was underlined as it was explained that the planet's warming trend is causing the climate to drastically change (paras. 7-10).

The point is getting beyond the oftentimes discombobulating debate about global warming wherein some assume that record-breaking cold temperatures or snowfall means that the globe isn't getting warmer. Modern-day civilization's dependence on sound bytes and social media has undoubtedly made this issue an arduous one to approach. Many people who live busy lives are easy targets for the ignorant attacks hurled at the science behind anthropogenic climate change. As a result, the doubt about the science is a product of its complex nature. Even so, giving up on them is not an option, because saving us from ourselves is an "all hands on deck" cause.

The scientific community understands the stakes here, and the statistics pertaining to their near-unanimity on the behavior of Earth's climate reinforces as much. For the rest of humanity lacking expertise in this field of study, it's difficult to reasonably overlook the fact that only three percent – as can be seen via NASA's website ("Consensus: 97% of climate scientists agree", n.d.) – of climate scientists disagree that humanity is causing climate change (para. 1). Let's put that into perspective, 3 out of 100 climate scientists is all the denialist movement has to support their intentional refusal to seize the moment. Would a rational man or woman be willing to bet his or her life when the odds of winning were 3 out of 100 tries?

Of course not, and we don't have to look too hard to see signs that the consensus is well-founded. Our home is changing at an ever-accelerating rate, and not for the better. Emily Atkin of ThinkProgress composed an article (Atkin, Emily, 2014) in which the shrinking ice cap on Mount Everest was discussed.

Elucidating the scientifically mind-boggling fact that the ice is melting from the typically reliably cold mountain tops of this region, it was noted that almost a fourth of the area's glaciers have disappeared in a mere three decades and that the glacial lake at the foot of Everest is "13 times bigger than it was [in the 1970s]" (paras. 4-6). At what point does it become clear that humanity must act as one to – at the very least – slow the pace of these changes?

What's important to remember is that human-caused climate change isn't just connected to the burning of fossil fuels. Rather, there are a number of other human activities influencing this shift and the dangers aren't limited to hotter summers and rising waters. One of these additional contributing factors is deforestation. Rebecca Lindsey reveals (Lindsey, Rebecca, 2007. para. 9) that "scientists [have estimated] that the [Amazon's] trees contain more carbon than 10 years worth of human-produced greenhouse gases" and that deforestation would return all of that to the atmosphere in a dangerously-short period of time. It's almost comparable to turning off the air conditioner and setting it on fire to heat the house even more.

Lindsey's reference to the Amazon, it should be remembered, is a mere warning about what would happen with the destruction of one rainforest. To be clear, humanity must act now to stop the ongoing deforestation in regions beyond South America. With approximately "half of the world's tropical forests [having] been cleared", according to Jessie Szalay (Szalay, Jessie, 2013) – as well as the fact that the destruction of forests has produced slightly less than one-fifth of the "[global annual] greenhouse gas emissions" -, we have deforestation to thank as a key factor in the current warming of our planet (paras. 1-2). Part of the challenge,

though, is in understanding why communities are clearing these trees.

While it may seem like a no-brainer to condemn a society for

deforestation, the growing demand for resources in an increasingly-globalized

economy puts a great deal of pressure on the most impoverished peoples to

provide the supply. Sometimes, deforestation – the article in LiveScience notes

(Szalay, Jessie, 2013) – spreads because the land previously cleared for other crop

use becomes too degraded over time from its improper use. Therefore, the farming

interests have to target other forests for destruction (para. 7). The issue of abusive

practices in agriculture will be discussed shortly, but it is important to point out

that a sustainable solution for agriculture and energy production is strongly

connected to the need to "save the rainforest [and all other forests]".

Forests are an essential component to the balance of life, and may well

hold keys to future advances. Jessie Szalay underlines (Szalay, Jessie, 2013) the

troubling fact that destroying forests for our selfish purposes harms both us – by

losing options for medical research – and the "[s]eventy percent of the world's

plants and animals [which inhabit them]" (para. 9). Yet another – and oftentimes

overlooked - problem caused by deforestation is the havoc that such wreaks on our

water cycle. The LiveScience article reminds us that trees, especially those in areas

like the afore-referenced Amazon, are crucial for "grounding the water in their

roots [before] releasing it into the atmosphere" and for ensuring that our climate

doesn't become too dry (para. 11).

Although climate change is the primary concern in this chapter, it is by no means the only concern. As mentioned before, the climate is strongly connected to the process by which we feed ourselves. After all, a chaotic climate shift defined by extremes makes it harder to manage the food supply. Along these lines, Miguel Altieri tells another troubling tale (Altieri, Miguel A., 2000) about how humanity's currently reckless push for "more" – mostly for profit – has corrupted our agricultural practices. He points out that the old-fashioned approach employing crop diversity and rotation as well as recycling animal waste – after feeding some of the crops to said animals – helped to tame pests and soil erosion. Now, the emergence of chemical fertilizer, new genetically-modified organisms, and monocultures – the massive fields of a single crop – have reversed the benefits of what worked before all in the name of the proverbial bottom line (paras. 1-3).

A truly united world, devoid of an obsession for making a "quick buck" could strike a proper balance between the needs to feed billions and the vital requirement that nature's needs are tended to at the same time. Returning to traditional agricultural techniques and encouraging a global cultural transformation wherein we learn to respect the seasons and the limitations thereof, eat mostly what is produced locally, and help the regions less fortunate in terms of food abundance will get us on a path towards sustainability. Creating artificial means for satisfying our insatiable desire to consume and enrich ourselves as we please may sound appealing in theory, but the consequences of putting such into practice far outweigh the fantastical perks. With respect to these consequences, it is likewise mentioned in the University of California, Berkeley article (Altieri,

Miguel A., 2000) that the wasteful chemical fertilizers pollute our groundwater

and eventually make their way to the open sea wherein they contribute to an

explosion in algae's numbers and create a negative domino effect of sorts for

numerous other marine species (paras. 9-10).

Humanity's impact on the Earth's oceans might be the most obvious and

depressing of all. Surface runoff – including the agricultural abuses just

highlighted -, oil spills, radiation leakage, and the deplorable dumping of garbage

all have ravaged this otherwise beautiful feature of our world. Moreover, National

Geographic alerts us ("Ocean Acidification: Carbon Dioxide Is Putting Shelled

Animals at Risk", n.d.) as to the impact that our carbon output is having on the

oceans. On the one hand, the oceans' absorbance of half the carbon that we have

produced has slowed the rate of climate change. Tragically, this has resulted in an

unnatural increase in the acidity level of our seas and is directly linked to the

endangerment of shelled animals due to the impact it has on their reproduction and

development (paras. 3-4). Yet again, we must come to terms with the fact that the

environment is not something that any individual person, community, or nation

can save. Instead, this is a challenge that requires unanimity.

Plain and simple, that unanimous effort requires a swift change in

behavior. In the mid-20th Century, there may have been sufficient time to

gradually phase-in alternative energy, but the dithering in the decades since has

left us with no choice other than a near-desperate leap to a cleaner future. To put

things in perspective, David Biello writes about (Biello, David, 2007) how

dependent contemporary society is on fossil fuels – especially when it comes to oil

– by noting that our fuel, electricity, and even food all utilize such. He underscores

the need to shift towards alternatives such as "plant-derived plastics" in order to

wean ourselves off of this destructive path (paras. 2-4). It is likewise mentioned

that our electric grid and approach to construction are in desperate need of an

environmentally-friendly modernization. By adopting "smart" technology and

employing renewable fuels, the carbon footprint relating to these can be reduced

tremendously (paras. 5, 7).

Just as mentioned earlier, the way we live – engrained in our culture –

must be altered in a sustainable manner. Mr. Biello looked into this issue by then

citing (Biello, David, 2007) how the trend of traveling far to one's workplace –

and other vital destinations – needs to be addressed. Between a boost in mass

transit, living near the worksite, an emphasis on walking and bike paths, as well as

"working from home", humanity can help both the environment and themselves

(paras. 9-10). Moreover, these methods – well, except the working at home option

– promote community and health; two major contributors to improved life

satisfaction.

Despite everything that has been discussed thus far, the conversation is

far from complete, because restoring the balance of nature isn't going to be

adequately dealt with until all the proverbial elephants in the room are

acknowledged. Though the *Scientific American* article discusses many other

important issues, overpopulation is a key topic tackled within. Yes, it may be

controversial to highlight this problem – as Biello does in advocating a "one child"

policy (Biello, David, 2007. paras. 26-28) -, since fears of genocide and infanticide rightly emerge. However, ignoring the connection between our finite, depleting

resources and the growing demand for more to support a massive population is to

be willfully delusional in regards to our ability in sustaining as much.

Bringing the global community together is the only option available if we

are at all serious about the environment. Reason being, that while one nation or

group of nations may decide to act, other - more desperate – nations might choose

to do nothing but to continue exploiting the Earth's resources purely because it

means economic growth and an elevated geopolitical stature. In an example of that

specific challenge, the Brookings Institution notes (Jones, Bruce et al, 2014) the

emerging power of China as well as how such affects the demand for oil; a

resource – also underscored by the article – of which the United States will soon

become the leading producer. Given this shift, and the weakness of certain global

institutions, it is mentioned that the current framework will demand a creative

coordination between America, Asia, and the G-20 to adequately govern energy

use and matters related to the climate (paras. 1, 4). Realistically, the plethora of

tasks ahead of us calls for more than twenty high-influential nations, for the entire

planet must be engaged in this campaign to preserve our home and our very

existence.

The way forward isn't without pain or controversy, and this fact must be

accepted before going any further. Many of us will not like the sacrifices to be

collectively and globally made, but the consequences of inaction involve

unimaginable pain for our descendants. An idea for managing our future

interaction with the environment – known as "sustainable development" –

emphasizes "meet[ing] the needs of the present without compromising the ability of future generations to meet their own needs", according to the International Institute for Sustainable Development ("What is Sustainable Development?", n.d., para. 2). Additionally, this line of thinking considers the entire planet as one unit, with all actions past and present having an affect on our future quality of life (paras. 3-5).

Life as we know it has reached its expiration date. The world in which we live, and from which we emerged and evolved, is not without its bounds. Earth will not live forever, and the lifestyle we take for granted has scarred our planetary mother in countless ways; some of which were not even mentioned in this chapter. To ensure that our species will have a fighting chance of not fading into the long list of extinct inhabitants, our resolve must be to change our habits and adapt according to the environment's needs and limitations.

First and foremost, a united front must be secured. No nation or community can be excluded, because there is a genuine risk that leaving anyone out will severely harm the powerless and only tilt the scales in favor of the opportunistic. Ultimately, exclusion exacerbates the problem and produces what amounts to a race to the bottom as each nation becomes hell-bent on exploiting as much as they can so as to not be the one left behind. To a degree, this is the path we are currently on, and it will do nothing but expedite our demise.

Lastly, humanity must finally recognize basic facts such as that global warming is real, that it is causing climate change, and that we have the power to slow this trend; even if the window of opportunity is closing with every month of inaction. Moreover, other troubling facts have to be acknowledged and addressed as well, such as the depletion of fresh water, the pollution of our water and air, and the need to tame population growth. Dealing with every one of these problems commands that we be united. This is especially important as far as the availability of fresh drinking water is concerned, as the solutions will be less than appealing for most and rather expensive in the long-term.

We are a stubborn, yet resourceful animal. Each successive generation of humans has seen us conquer one challenge after another through our unity and innovative spirit. There is no reason to believe that striking a proper balance with the environment is beyond our reach, because we have never known a problem that we were content with not solving. Saving ourselves from self-destruction is within reach, just as saving ourselves from illness was through the advent and evolution of medical science. This is why the next topic pertains to the future of medical research.

References:

Altieri, M.A. (2000, July 30). Modern Agriculture: Ecological impacts and the

possibilities for truly sustainable farming. The University of California,
Berkeley

website. Retrieved April 26, 2014, from:

http://nature.berkeley.edu/~miguel-alt/modern_agriculture.html

Atkin, E. (2014, April 25). Why Mount Everest Is Shrinking. *Thinkprogress.org*.

Retrieved May 1, 2014, from:

http://thinkprogress.org/climate/2014/04/25/3430809/everest-is-

shrinking/?utm_medium=twitter&utm_source=twitterfeed

Biello, D. (2007, November 26). 10 Solutions for Climate Change. *Scientific
American*

on the web. Retrieved April 21, 2014, from:

http://www.scientificamerican.com/article/10-solutions-for-climate-
change/

Consensus: 97% of climate scientists agree. (n.d.). National Aeronautics and
Space

Administration website. Retrieved April 23, 2014, from:

http://climate.nasa.gov/scientific-consensus

Jones, B., O'Brien, E., & Steven, D. (2014, April 15). Fueling a new order? The
new

geopolitical and security consequences of energy. The Brookings
Institution

website. Retrieved April 22, 2014, from:

http://www.brookings.edu/research/papers/2014/04/14-geopolitical-security-energy-jones-steven

Lindsey, R. (2007, March 30). Tropical Deforestation. National Aeronautics and Space

Administration website. Retrieved April 28, 2014, from:

http://earthobservatory.nasa.gov/Features/Deforestation/

Ocean Acidification: Carbon Dioxide Is Putting Shelled Animals at Risk. (n.d.). National

Geographic website. Retrieved April 27, 2014, from:

http://ocean.nationalgeographic.com/ocean/critical-issues-ocean-acidification/

Szalay, J. (2013, March 6). Deforestation: Facts, Causes & Effects. Livescience.com.

Retrieved April 24, 2014, from: http://www.livescience.com/27692-deforestation.html

What is climate change? (n.d.) State of Washington, Department of Ecology website.

Retrieved April 29, 2014, from:

http://www.ecy.wa.gov/climatechange/whatis.htm

What is Sustainable Development? (n.d.). International Institute for Sustainable

Development website. Retrieved April 30, 2014, from:

http://www.iisd.org/sd/

Section Three: Science

Chapter Eight: Controversial Medical Research

Chapter Eight: Controversial Medical Research

The past two or three centuries have transformed humanity a great deal.

Much of this transformation occurred during the Twentieth Century, seeing an end

to traditional colonialism, the rise of global organizations aimed at fostering peace,

and even realizing a once-unimaginable feat of setting foot on the moon. Another,

sometimes overlooked, accomplishment of the previous century was the leap in

our life expectancy. While a number of factors contributed to this amazing turn of

events, nothing did more to boost our longevity than the advancements in medical

science. With an eye towards the immediate and distant future, the potential for

what humanity can achieve through medical science must be pondered through the

lens of unity and a willingness to let go of our squeamishness.

In order to push the proverbial envelope of what our species is capable of,

we ought to not rule out any research based on archaic mindsets and onerous

restrictions. For instance, it is possible for cancer and other major ailments to be

cured and for our life expectancy to be expanded further, but the narrow focus

forced upon us by bans on substances such as marijuana and on embryonic stem

cell research severely undercuts what we can achieve. So, marijuana, genetics, and

the varying controversial research options in between will be highlighted here to

argue that humanity needs to be able to evaluate and possibly unlock the secrets

contained within each research field. Who knows what the coming century holds

for us should we ultimately decide to do what's our right to do as a species in the

perpetual evolutionary campaign to pass on our genes to the next generation?

Up through the current age, humankind has conquered a long list of

previously horrifying medical nightmares. Keep in mind that people used to die in large numbers from the common cold, from influenza, from polio, and from

tuberculosis; to name a few. Not only that, but getting what now amounts to a

flesh wound in battle was once almost a sure death sentence as many soldiers who

died in wars past died from preventable deaths due to the poor condition of their

medical treatment. In many families, it was once an accepted part of life that a

number of your newborns wouldn't survive infancy; that is, if they even survived

the birth to begin with. Today, thanks to the once-unyielding pursuit of the best

solutions that medical science could discover, our species is no longer damned to

an easy demise in any of those examples.

While advances continue to be made even now, there are a set of

unnecessary obstacles to our research. First among these roadblocks are the

prohibitions against certain substances, such as marijuana. This is an arbitrary

restriction made out of choice, not necessity, and the possible medical

breakthroughs which may be opened up to us as a result of studying marijuana for

its positive effects are being denied to us for no logical reason other than the greed

of those interests benefiting from its continued illegality. One article – found at the

Collective Evolution website (Walia, Arjun, 2013) – offers an argument in favor

of cancer being combated with the chemicals found in this particular plant. The

author claims that marijuana can trigger a positive chemical reaction in the body

which may either significantly reduce the spread of cancer cells or extinguish them

altogether (para. 3).

A number of officials who once took a stance in staunch opposition to the

use of marijuana for any reason – including medical research – have come to recognize it as a potential goldmine for future treatments. For instance, in explaining his reasoning for coming to support marijuana's legalization, Doctor Sanjay Gupta (Gupta, Sanjay, 2013) talked about a little girl he met whose seizures had been reduced from "300 a week" to "2 or 3 per month" by integrating medical marijuana into her medicinal program (para. 7). He also notes how the prohibition of marijuana gained teeth via an influential letter written by a former Assistant Secretary of Health, whom wrote that this particular substance had to be set at "Schedule 1" because there wasn't enough known about it (paras. 11-13). Sounds counterintuitive, doesn't it?

What also sounds contrary to what commonsense would lead us to believe is the notion that viruses can be helpful. Yet, there are plenty of examples wherein a virus has worked in our favor. If not for the manipulation of viruses and the intentional injection of such into our bloodstreams and airways, vaccinations would not be possible. Having said that, the ongoing conspiracy theory-based movement against vaccination is worrisome as it preys on those whose trust in institutions is already weak for a variety of reasons and it convinces them that the campaign to inoculate is somehow a secret plot to poison and control the population. Perhaps for that reason alone, this nonsensical backlash against a successful medical scientific achievement, further exploration into what meddling with viruses can offer us will be met with some needless controversy.

Our greatest health challenge in the modern age is in pursuing a cure for cancer. Alexander Masters (Masters, Alexander, 2012) shares a story about one professor named Magnus Essand who helped discover a means of potentially eradicating cancer by way of using viral infections to our benefit. By manipulating the function of a virus, the cancer becomes the target of an all-out assault. In the mice that have been tested with this method, the targeted tumors "melt[ed] away". Since cancer cells don't self-destruct like healthy cells do, the virus can latch-on and do its work before spreading to other cancer cells. The *Telegraph* article actually reminds us that doctors have known for quite some time that viruses can be an effective enemy for cancer, but that the mastery of genetics – which is, in and of itself, a matter for separate discussion momentarily - has only been in our grasp for a few decades (paras. 2-3, 6, 15-17).

If you're not one to patiently wait for the day when we can program viruses to do our bidding, then another story should capture your interest. Researchers from the world-renown Mayo Clinic, *USA Today* reports (Seavert, Lindsey, 2014), conducted a successful test on one patient wherein the measles vaccine was applied – with enough of a dosage to vaccinate ten million people (para. 1) – and apparently cured her previously-"incurable blood cancer". A single shot of the vaccine demonstrated the promise that this approach may have by causing the immune system – as in the other example – to target the otherwise covert cancer cells (paras. 1-2, 6). While this is also a tactic currently in development, it goes to show that our options for meeting the global task of mitigating or extinguishing cancer aren't limited to just a few. Again, the first hurdle we must overcome is the controversy surrounding such methods.

Over the past two decades, few areas of medical science have generated more controversy than stem cell research; with most of that heated debate focusing on the use of discarded embryos. What's this all about? A "Stem Cell Research

Facts" website reveals ("What is a Stem Cell?", n.d.) that a stem cell is basically a

cell without a designated function in the body. Naturally, this cell type gets

programmed to "becom[e] another more differentiated cell type in the body".

Through humanity's advances in understanding and manipulating the molecular

level of life, we may be able to use these cells to address a whole host of health

issues (paras. 1-2). Sounds innocent enough, right? Consider that this research has

much to offer humankind.

Thinking back to the threat of cancer, stem cell research has already

given us a wealth of knowledge as to how we can confront such. Remarkably, part

of what we've learned through this research is what leads to cancer in the first

place. Charlie Cooper of *The Independent* shared a story (Cooper, Charlie, 2014)

with a hint of hope in it by reporting a recent discovery of "cancer stem cells"

which could hold the key to "eradicat[ing targeted cancers] altogether". Basically,

the research has opened a new door into understanding how cancer develops

(paras. 1-4, 6-7). Obviously, if we can figure out the ingredients to cancer, then

treating it or curing it becomes much easier.

Another benefit of stem cell research is far more controversial – for

whatever reason – since it involves the use of discarded human eggs. As I alluded

to before, embryonic stem cell research is a hot topic particularly for those who

claim that its practice destroys life for the sake of science. Similar and related to

that issue is concern about anything involving cloning. Even so, the combination

of cloning and stem cell research – via adult, not embryonic, stem cells – has provided a possible additional weapon in our arsenal against premature death.

Elizabeth Landau reported (Landau, Elizabeth, 2014) that cloning has recently

been effective in creating new adult stem cells by "fertilizing" an egg with the

nucleus of a particular cell type (paras. 1-3). Honestly, this is only controversial

because of a lack of education as to what constitutes a living being, as well as the

fact that many believe it to be inappropriate for life to be reproduced by humanity

in any way, shape, or form.

Cloning - the act of replicating a specimen - is a highly controversial

topic. While this book does not advocate for humans to be cloned in whole, our

justifiable ethical and moral concerns about doing so are needlessly hindering us

from using selective cloning to our advantage. By dispensing with moral

absolutism – a subject for further discussion in a later chapter -, we can unite to

find what this medical science tool has to offer. Is it really necessary for us to

continue tying our hands?

Besides, cloning isn't as manmade as the fanatics would have you

believe. The National Human Genome Research Institute's website reveals

("Cloning", n.d.) that cloning actually happens in nature by way of "asexual

reproduction" or when "a fertilized egg splits" thus resulting in identical siblings

(paras. 3-4). It goes on to point out that cloning has been used to create sheep that

produce milk more beneficial for human blood clotting concerns (para. 23). Yet

another potential benefit is that embryos could be cloned for the purpose of

studying diseases and learning how best to treat them (para. 28). Additionally, future doctors could use cloning to make healthy organs from our own DNA, thereby eliminating the need for finding a suitable organ donor.

The extension of humanity's lifespan over the course of time has primarily been due to what medical science has accomplished. Thanks to the hard work of these scientists, more of us now survive birth, childhood, and adolescence than ever before. In the abstract of a report found on the Centers for Disease Control website (Kochanek, Kenneth D. et al, 2013. pg. 1), the average life expectancy for Americans as of 2010 was 78.7 years. Before medical science, achieving such an age was a privilege for the select few in each society, and it was almost impossible for impoverished humans to realize. Now, there is some credible talk of helping our species reach an average century-long existence, and science could permit such to occur through genetic research.

To envision this potential medical milestone, we should first entertain the fantasy that our descendants will one day dispense with death altogether. In highlighting the discovery of a jellyfish which possesses the ability to theoretically live forever – by regressing to a cellular level and starting over again, all when the environment becomes "unfavorable" -, Nikki Kong assures us that an eternal physical life is a real possibility (Kong, Nikki R., 2013. paras. 2-3). A key component, according to Kong, to extending our life expectancies is in dealing with aging. To deal with that, studies have found that an appropriate balance of metabolism – which apparently gets siphoned off for use in reproduction – is where the answer seems to lie (paras. 4-11). Basically, the very natural process which allows a species to ensure its overall survival - procreation – is our worst

enemy as an individual.

Genetic research could allow us to live longer by helping us slow - or

even reverse - the aging process itself. One study – published in an article via *The*

Wall Street Journal (Naik, Gautam, 2010) – successfully conducted an experiment

wherein boosting mice "telomere" levels reversed the aging process and made

older mice appear and function as young adults. According to the science behind

the study, telomeres erode over time thusly triggering the degradation of cell and

bodily functions (paras. 4, 7-9, 14-15). If we can somehow figure out how to

safely maintain a stable telomere level, humans could prolong our youth

significantly, if not indefinitely.

Going forward, humanity may never actually conquer what is known as

the "great equalizer". We should at least expect that medical science, when

permitted to evolve devoid of ridiculous obstacles and with a united focus to

improve the quality of life, has much more to offer in the decades and centuries

ahead. Unless we allow scientists to responsibly use all of what nature and our

knowledge thereof has to offer, then what we are doing is intentionally choosing to

stagnate as a species. Never before in the history of the world, or maybe even the

cosmos, has any species done more than humanity to hinder its evolution. Maybe,

just maybe, that's because our general collective understanding of evolution itself

is sorely lacking. That's why our next chapter will emphasize the need to unite

around the cause of properly educating all peoples about our natural origins.

References:

Cloning. (n.d.). National Human Genome Research Institute website. Retrieved May 21,

2014, from: http://www.genome.gov/25020028

Cooper, C. (2014, May 15). First evidence of cancer stem cells brings hope for possible

future treatment. *The Independent on the web*. Retrieved May 25, 2014, from:

http://www.independent.co.uk/life-style/health-and-families/health-
news/first-evidence-of-cancer-stem-cells-brings-hope-for-possible-future-
treatment-9380201.html

Gupta, S. (2013, August 8). Why I changed my mind on weed. *CNN on the web*.

Retrieved May 23, 2014, from:

http://www.cnn.com/2013/08/08/health/gupta-changed-mind-marijuana/

Kochanek, K.D., Murphy, S.L., & Xu, J. (2013, May 8). Deaths: Final data for 2010.

National Vital Statistics Reports, 61(4), 1-99. Retrieved May 25, 2014, from:

http://www.cdc.gov/nchs/data/nvsr/nvsr61/nvsr61_04.pdf

Kong, N.R. (2013, April 22). Chasing Immortality. *Berkeley Science Review on the web*.

Retrieved May 20, 2014, from:

http://sciencereview.berkeley.edu/article/chasing-immortality/

Landau, E. (2014, April 28). Cloning used to make stem cells from adult humans.

CNN

on the web. Retrieved May 22, 2014, from:

http://www.cnn.com/2014/04/28/health/stem-cell-breakthrough/

Masters, A. (2012, August 31). A virus that kills cancer: the cure that's waiting in

the

cold. *The Telegraph on the web*. Retrieved May 18, 2014, from:

http://www.telegraph.co.uk/health/healthnews/9508895/A-virus-that-

kills-cancer-the-cure-thats-waiting-in-the-coldc.html

Naik, G. (2010, November 28). Aging Ills Reversed in Mice. *The Wall Street

Journal on*

the web. Retrieved May 24, 2014, from:

http://online.wsj.com/news/articles/SB100014240527487037857045 7564

2964209242180?mod=googlenews_wsj&mg=reno64-

wsj&url=http%3A%2F%2Fonline.wsj.com%2Farticle%2FSB100014240

52748703785704575642964209242180.html%3Fmod%3Dgooglenews_

wsj

Seavert, L. (2014, May 15). Massive dose of measles vaccine clears woman's

cancer.

USA Today on the web. Retrieved May 27, 2014, from:

http://www.usatoday.com/story/news/nation-now/2014/05/15/measles-

vaccine-cancer-mayo-clinic/9115363/

Walia, A. (2013, August 23). 20 Medical Studies That Prove Cannabis Can Cure

Cancer.

collective-evolution.com website. Retrieved May 17, 2014, from:

http://www.collective-evolution.com/2013/08/23/20-medical-studies-that-

prove-cannabis-can-cure-cancer/

What is a Stem Cell? (n.d.). StemCellResearchFacts.org website. Retrieved May

19,

2014, from: http://www.stemcellresearchfacts.org/what-is-a-stem-cell/

Section Three: Science

Chapter Nine: Evolution

Chapter Nine: Evolution

Evolution is a word which – unlike any other individual word in the modern world – triggers a deeply impassioned, and oftentimes irrational, argument upon its very utterance. This is a curious fact since the theory of evolution is a product of our scientific curiosity as a species. Humanity's search for answers has led us down a path with many twists and turns in addition to roadblocks set up by those who would prefer to not question their antiquated belief system by proceeding further or even accepting how far we've already come. While the pushback against scientific discovery is as traditional as the myths which inspire said pushback, there must come a time when we prioritize the need to learn more over the desire to live in denial.

As a whole, we human beings could benefit tremendously by promoting unity in thought and purpose; especially as far as our understanding of how the natural world we all take for granted came to be. People in every region have to be exposed to these facts of life, because ignorance anywhere threatens our collective progress. While religion will be discussed at length in the next chapter it is important to remember the role it plays in restraining our unity. If we are serious about coming together and moving forward, then the intellectual barriers – established and maintained by our primitive thinking - have to be removed.

When Mr. Darwin published his book outlining the natural process of evolution, he no doubt knew that he would be confronted with a monumental public backlash the likes of which had not been seen since Isaac Newton offered his theory about gravity. Then again, considering that Darwin's theory pertained to the origin of life as we know it, the threat it posed to the dogmatic status quo was more significant than any other scientific theory which had preceded it. After all,

religions are born when humans attempt to explain the purpose for our existence.

If life is merely a consequence of having the right conditions – such as the type of

planet we inhabit, whether it occupies an orbit in the so-called "goldilocks zone",

and whether the right elements are present – over a span of billions of years, then

all those stories about a deity or a pantheon of numerous deities creating and

periodically testing us for whatever reason are no more than creations of our

amazing collective imaginations. Evolution isn't just a revolutionary scientific

theory; it's the key to dismantling religion's very foundation.

Part of the pushback against Darwin has been the attempt by his

detractors to assert that there just hasn't been enough time for evolution to produce

the diversity of life we see on Earth today. Though many believers have since

abandoned the ludicrous "Young Earth" theory – with its literal interpretation of

the Christian Bible and the planet's age that one supposedly calculates therewith -,

it poses an intellectual hurdle as humans have struggled for more than a century to

accept the scientific fact about Earth being roughly 4.5 billion years old. This

debate – as Dennis O'Neil details (O'Neil, Dennis, n.d.) – has always been a hotly

contested aspect of evolution by those who refuse to accept such. For the people

who dare not question what the fundamentalist religious view of Earth's history

says, the notion that Mother Earth – let alone the universe – is billions of years old

is unacceptable. Consider that there was even initial resistance to acknowledge

that prehistoric tools had been located near prehistoric animals. Instead of being

products of our ancestors' contemporary genius, to the deniers these were stones created by powerful strikes of lightning (paras. 21, 23-26). Simply put, evolution has always been opposed by the closed-minded because it – like the planet's real age – forces one to contemplate life outside of what their respective religion has taught them.

Ultimately, that's what it all comes down to, what we are taught to believe. That's why some within the anti-evolution movement are attempting to circumvent secular requirements in education by advocating for the teaching of "intelligent design". The intelligent design theory – the history of which is discussed in an article published in the *Natural History* magazine (Behe, Michael J. et al, 2002) – has roots spanning at least two centuries to the "English theologian William Paley" who claimed that nature's complexity – like that of a pocket watch – can't be the result of anything but the intentional act of some intelligent being. Even as most of the scientific community has come to accept Darwin's theory of evolution, a revival of this undoubtedly religion-driven "theory" – promoted by some "academics with scientific credentials" – has sparked an intellectual firestorm wherein science has been forced to defend itself against this encroachment by religion (paras. 1-3).

This pseudo-scientific alternative to evolution is primarily dependent on attempting to cherry-pick what its proponents claim to be holes in Darwin's theory, but the scientific community easily refutes those claims and responds by highlighting the problems found within "intelligent design". One example of a flaw found with the intelligent design "theory" – as pointed out in the *Natural History* article (Behe, Michael J. et al, 2002) – is that the proponents thereof often try to claim that certain functions are "irreducibly complex", in that they can't be regressed to a previous state without ceasing to function. The flaw here is that it ignores what other functions could be performed when removing the supposedly "essential" parts. After all, part of how organisms evolve is that they adapt their functionality to meet new challenges or they develop entirely new functions via mutation (para. 12).

What doesn't make matters any better is that it seems easier to say that every living thing was "created" as opposed to the reality; which happens to be far more complicated than a simple abracadabra moment by some mythical omnipotent force. The simplicity of creation or "intelligent design" makes it a more appealing explanation for those who either don't understand or don't want to understand the science behind evolution. For that reason, it is imperative that science classes make evolution as easy to understand as possible for the younger, more impressionable, minds. If evolution is easy to comprehend for a middle school science student, then that student is less likely to later reject such in favor of a non-scientific alternative. For reasons to be touched on later, reaching people before they get seduced by the superstitions of our ancestors is a crucial component to the unity of humankind.

Thankfully, evolution isn't all that difficult to teach. A special article published on the University of Cambridge's website (Montgomery, Stephen, 2009) simplifies the theory of evolution by explaining one of its most basic concepts: natural selection. Stephen Montgomery explains that species evolve by passing on characteristic "variations" which enhance the chance for survival and reproduction. Eventually, these empowering traits get "spread through[out] the

population" as time slowly unfolds. Another part of the equation is that this

change mostly occurs at a snail's pace – metaphorically speaking – as it involves

minor mutations and adaptations over a period of time until one species becomes

two or more (paras. 1-3). The article also points out that Charles Darwin observed

the reproductive and competitive behavior between and within species. Basically,

a species – as part of its survival instincts – produces a surplus of offspring to

enhance the chances of its ability to pass on beneficial genes and so as to give it an

advantage in the broader competition for Earth's limited resources (para. 6).

In addition to making evolution easier to understand, science classes the

world over should aim to underline the theory's beautiful and awe-inspiring

nature. Students ought to be encouraged to think of the transformations of life as

being amazing or "cool", because they are. Much focus should be devoted to the

variety in elephant and horse species – to name a few – so as to show how far

these animals have come in the past million or so years. An entire section of

evolutionary instruction could even highlight the origins of whales and dolphins.

Curious as it may be, the evolution of mammals in the sea created a bit of

a headache for Mr. Darwin. The original draft of Darwin's world-changing book

on evolution offered – according to LiveScience (Than, Ker, 2012) – a

hypothetical example of a bear-like whale evolving from those bears who fish by

swimming with an open mouth. Though this idea was more or less laughed off by

his peers, he wasn't far off from the means by which mammals ended up in the

water. As it turns out, examining cows and the hippopotamus was much closer to being accurate as well as believable (paras. 4-8). Perhaps one of the most awe-inspiring facts about the whale's development is that its blowhole moved from being a facial nostril to the top of its head so as to enable the animal to remain partially submerged while getting a breath of air (paras. 17-18). The potential for the whale's evolutionary history to captivate young people can not be denied.

Truthfully, the evolution of mammals alone can consume at least an entire year's worth of material in a class devoted to evolutionary science. The wonderful documentation – courtesy of the fossil record - of how prehistoric mammalian species gave rise to the creatures we know and love today promises to inspire a hunger for exploring more about what Mother Nature has given us and what it may yet still contribute in the coming centuries and millennia. Central to this instruction, though, is the acceptance that we humans are not somehow separated from evolution. In fact, humanity's youth needs to welcome our origins with open arms and be open to the thought that evolution is likely not finished with us.

In covering an ongoing debate about how or whether evolution is actively affecting humanity, Olly Bootle of *BBC News* (Bootle, Olly, 2011) notes that the presence of our various "races" and the change in our metabolism are obvious clues that we are still evolving. The fact that humans couldn't digest lactose prior to agriculture's invention, and that lactose tolerance is radically different in communities with long traditions of dairy farms compared to those with a limited experience therewith provides more than sufficient evidence for the continued influence of evolution in our existence (paras. 7, 9-11). Human evolution has also been affected by "sexual selection" – a feature that is crucial for the evolution of

fish and birds, Elizabeth Pennisi notes (Pennisi, Elizabeth, 2012) -, as is observed

by looking at the mate-choosing and procreation patterns of certain individuals. If

a person is having more luck than their peers at passing their genes on to the next

generation by marrying more often or marrying the "right" mate, then that is the

very essence of natural selection at work (paras. 1-3, 5, 7).

    While it is impossible to predict the impact that evolution will have on us

in the distant future, we can keep an eye out for clues as to changes that we are

currently experiencing. Interestingly, one study – also discussed in Bootle's article

(Bootle, Olly, 2011) – hints that humanity may be getting shorter and heavier. This

may or may not be a temporary trend, and could be limited to some advanced

communities (paras. 20-23), but it is an eye-opening observation nonetheless.

Considering all that we know about our recent adaptations, it isn't entirely

fantastical to suggest that our species could – in time - be the first in the history of

Earth to guide or even mitigate its own evolution.

    Before such can ever be achieved, though, we must get a handle on the

teaching of evolutionary science to the young. Students in every nation should be

exposed to this important subject to both stifle problematic – even disruptive –

ignorance as well as to encourage a substantial percentage of them to pick up the

proverbial torch of scientific discovery as they come of age. With millions,

possibly billions, of adolescent humans being sheltered from learning about

evolution, our species is utilizing only a fraction of our intellectual potential.

Tragically, this willful ignorance is currently being perpetuated in more advanced nations such as the United States as the fundamentalists in certain religious corners

desperately shield countless children from the truth. Furthermore, these hyper-

religious forces are trying to exacerbate the problem by pushing for schools to

teach their "alternatives" – including the barely distinguishable creationist and

"intelligent design" approaches - to evolution.

So why can't we allow the teaching of "intelligent design" – or even

creationism, for that matter - in our science classes? As the National Academy of

Sciences illustrates ("Intelligent Design", n.d.), it's because this "theory" is an

anti-science position to start with. Reason being, that it is derived from an

unyielding, un-amendable, and un-testable belief system. In contrast, evolution has

been subjected to and has withstood the intense scrutiny of the scientific

community for over a century. Science leaves no wiggle room for unjustified

beliefs, because one person or a few people's reluctance to challenge their ideas

will not stop their peers from doing so and subjecting the failings thereof to the

court of community judgment (paras. 6-9).

Undeterred by these inconvenient facts of how science really works, the

fundamentalists continue in their push for indoctrination. To them, evolution is

debatable on faith-based grounds, thus rendering the science irrelevant. That's

why one of their favorite attacks against "evolutionists" or "Darwinists" is to

assert that evolution itself requires one to have "faith" in such having transpired.

Why debate the science when you can just create a new debate forum altogether

for the issue? On this front, a disturbing number of people without a comprehensive understanding of evolutionary science fall victim to the persuasive arguments of those in denial.

What's intriguing about the evolution debate is that – as John Farrell says (Farrell, John, 2014) – the majority of us haven't even been paying attention to the real controversy: which is most responsible for our evolution out of "random" and "selective" "changes"? Apparently, this discussion has been raging for decades and is full of wonder and a bit of drama as some refuse to admit that anything but natural selection has steered the emergence of modern life (paras. 1-4). If humanity can dispense with the distractions long enough to embrace what science has to offer, this particular aspect of evolutionary science could inspire future students to get involved in the scientific community. Just imagine how exciting it could make a science class to highlight this genuine debate on evolution. Truth is, some kid – or group of kids – alive or born today could resolve this debate once and for all!

A united educational standard both hinders the corrosive effects of confusion and ensures that our species can continue to move forward by leaps and bounds as we search for answers. Additionally, a more comprehensive grasp of evolution could enable future generations to master the affects thereof. By fostering a more scientific-friendly environment on evolution, humanity enhances its ability to identify possible threats to our survival. An example of how this is already being explored is in how one *Cornell Chronicle* study (Ramanujan, Krishna, 2005) used what we know about human evolution in the past five million years to zero-in on and detect potential hereditary diseases – such as muscular dystrophy – by tracking the "deleterious or harmful mutations" of certain genes

(paras. 3-7). Why allow these opportunities to pass us by in favor of clinging to a

debate which attempts to sidestep science altogether?

Is it easy to admit when you're wrong? No, especially when the point

you're arguing is something about which you are passionate. However, it is time

for universal acceptance of the truth that is evolution. Will this debate go away

easily? Doubtfully, and we have blind devotion to religion to thank for that.

Accordingly, a pathway to liberating humankind from the blanket tyranny of faith

must be charted, and the next chapter will focus on just that.

References:

Behe, M.J., Dembski, W.A., Forrest, B., Maestro, V., Miller, K.R., Milner, R., Pennock,

    R.T., Scott, E.C., & Wells, J. (2002, April). Intelligent Design? *Natural*

History.

    Retrieved June 11, 2014, from:

    http://www.actionbioscience.org/evolution/nhmag.html

Bootle, O. (2011, February 28). Are humans still evolving by Darwin's natural selection?

    BBC News on the web. Retrieved June 12, 2014, from:

    http://www.bbc.com/news/science-environment-12535647

Farrell, J. (2014, February 27). The Real Evolution Debate: Is It All Just Natural

    Selection? *Forbes on the web*. Retrieved June 17, 2014, from:

    http://www.forbes.com/sites/johnfarrell/2014/02/27/the-real-evolution-

    debate-is-it-all-just-natural-selection/

Intelligent Design. (n.d.). The National Academy of Sciences website. Retrieved June 14,

    2014, from: http://www.nas.edu/evolution/IntelligentDesign.html

Montgomery, S. (2009). Natural Selection. Christ's College, University of Cambridge

    website. Retrieved June 12, 2014, from:

    http://darwin200.christs.cam.ac.uk/pages/index.php?page_id=d3

O'Neil, D. (n.d.). Darwin and Natural Selection. Palomar College website.
Retrieved

June 13, 2014, from: http://anthro.palomar.edu/evolve/evolve_2.htm

Pennisi, E. (2012, May 1). Signals of Natural Selection Found in Recent Human

Evolution. Wired.com website. Retrieved June 16, 2014, from:

http://www.wired.com/2012/05/human-genetic-evolution/

Ramanujan, K. (2005, October 19). Natural selection has strongly influenced
recent

human evolution, Cornell/Celera Genomics study finds. *Cornell
Chronicle on the*

web. Retrieved June 14, 2014, from:

http://www.news.cornell.edu/stories/2005/10/natural-selection-has-

strongly-influenced-recent-human-evolution

Than, K. (2012, December 7). What is Darwin's Theory of Evolution?
LiveScience.com

website. Retrieved June 13, 2014, from: http://www.livescience.com/474-

controversy-evolution-works.html

Section Three: Science

Chapter Ten: Agnosticism and Secularism

Chapter Ten: Agnosticism and Secularism

Let there be no misunderstanding about what is to be discussed in the coming paragraphs; this is far from the easiest obstacle to unity that we must overcome. Initially, this chapter was going to be entitled "Religion". However, upon further consideration, it became clear that such a chapter within a section devoted exclusively to scientific matters would be counterintuitive. Instead, while the primary focus of this chapter may be related to matters of religion, the proceeding argument contained within merely only touches on such through the lens of what science can permit the collective to reasonably adopt.

In an ideal world, religion can be safely kept out of the public sphere. This is because one's religious beliefs are - first and foremost - private. Realistically, the relationship between the state and religion is not so extricable. The propensity for religiously-inspired passions to impel activism both good and bad casts a significant degree of doubt as to a society's ability to honestly claim a fealty to the principle of secularism so long as blind faith is countenanced. For this reason, what follows here is an argument which aims to underline how modern secularism divides humanity and which attempts to make the case for an agnostic state as the only rational path towards unity.

To completely grasp why the secular approach is the more divisive, one must first consider the origins thereof. What was it that necessitated the separation of state and religion? As will be discussed in more detail shortly, safeguarding state and religion from one another was seen as a crucial component in the development of a democracy by promoting the freedoms of thought and dissent. This framework would only remain sustainable for as long as such a democracy would maintain religious homogeneity or if the religious views of the participants in no way influenced their political activity.

Prior to the establishment of guaranteed rights to free thought, civilization had most always been constructed around a centralized manner of thinking pertaining to morals, law, and questions of origin. The earliest recorded civilizations were united by myths derived from their polytheism, which – in turn – was used to legitimize the status quo. Humankind's lack of scientific understanding in our then-primitive intellectual nature fostered and almost demanded this very societal arrangement. Otherwise, devoid of a unifying message or mission, our species would have never progressed beyond our initial hunter-gatherer phase.

While a great many horrors were committed for the sake of pleasing these mythical forces, there can be no denying that achievements like the rule of law were aided as a result of our experimentation with imaginary realms of omnipotent, omniscient masters. Absent the pagan justifications for unifying early humans around a common purpose and cause, there is no likely alternative scenario wherein our intellectual evolution – via the advent of writing, mathematics, and science – could have been given a starting platform. Could even philosophy have emerged in a world without the plethora of diverse pantheons? Possibly, but with whom would they have shared their epiphanies if there had never been a common language; as motivated by the primitive active imaginations of our ancestors?

As the polytheistic empires began to fade away and eventually succumb to the popular uprising of monotheism – via Christianity, and later Islam -, the notions of freedom and social justice began to take root. Truthfully, the structure of society hardly changed at all with the shift from belief in many gods to one. After all, there remained a caste system which successfully kept the impoverished from rising up primarily by promising the downtrodden something greater in the afterlife. Meanwhile, the elite class was preserved via requirements for peasants to respect their authority and to pay them a tax of some sort, such as tithes.

Rome's fall undoubtedly stalled humankind's forward thrust, but only because superstition dominated as the people of Europe were divided and temporarily dispensed with their intellectual exploration. Centuries of conflict with Muslims over the Iberian Peninsula and the "Holy Land" created longstanding cultural wounds that are still visible to this today. The Black Plague nearly wiped out the Eastern Hemisphere's human population, and its carnage was irrationally blamed on the Jewish people by fundamentalist blood-thirsty factions such as the Flagellants in one of the most horrendous chapters in human history involving the slaughter of countless innocents for supposedly "poisoning the well". Ironically, the culture which did the most to both safeguard humanity's accomplishments up to that time and even advance such a little further is the same culture now perceived to be the most in need of modernizing: the Muslims.

Regardless of what one religious culture or another positively contributed to humanity's progress, the atrocities committed in the name of promoting one theocracy's objectives over another make it clear that policies derived from anything but facts tends to be tyrannical. No nation or group of nations should understand this better than the United States and the continents of North and South America. Yes, religion influenced the maps of the Eastern Hemisphere, but the "discovery" and subsequent conquest of North and South America was motivated in large part by a European mission to convert the "savage" native inhabitants of these strange lands to their particular brand of Christianity. Throw in the quest for precious metals and an enlarged empire – as well as cheap labor to exploit along the way – and you have the perfect ingredients for the many New World-based crimes against humanity perpetrated in the name of "God".

With the United States, the origins of this country are directly linked to the tumultuous religious history of its former imperial master: England. Before the American Revolution, the American English colonists were accustomed to the unstable nature of England's state religion. With one monarch, you had to adhere to Catholicism, but the next could very well force you to convert to Anglicanism – the Church of England, as created by King Henry the VIII when the Pope wouldn't permit him to divorce his wife for his mistress -, and so on. Additionally, many colonists fled Europe either because of religious persecution or because their European homeland wasn't strict enough. Either way, one can not extricate the quest for religious freedom from the fabric of American life.

Upon securing their independence from the English Crown and its theocratic ways, America's "Founding Fathers" took a truly unprecedented act: establishing a legitimate form of government with religion and state kept separate. It is no accident that the very first line in the First Amendment – which effectively guarantees the right to free thinking – is a protection for the people from the volatile nature of theocracy. When a government can dictate how their citizens should think there can be no dissent, and if dissent is absent then democracy can not exist. In this respect, the children of the Age of Enlightenment – such as America's Framers – were correct to create the world's first secular state, because it is not the business of government to direct the collective's thinking. Instead, government's only role in this respect should be to insure that the people have adequate access to the facts so as to promote an informed electorate.

For little more than a century and a half, America's experiment with secularism was largely without incident. The turning point for Western Secularism was the Red Scare, which – in its second wave following World War Two – was marked by the American government engaging in a fierce domestic and worldwide propaganda war against the Soviet Union. Part of that campaign involved references to the Soviets as being "godless" – an obviously intentional attack on the Soviet character - due to their official state atheism. To any predominantly Christian or otherwise religious nation, this was meant to make Marxism less appealing and even seemingly evil.

With McCarthyism in the air, and the Western governments – led by America – decrying Russia's ostensible aversion to the faithful, the only logical reaction at the time seemed to be a reversal of the secular in favor of the theocratic. It was with this hyper-religious rhetoric that the American government essentially compelled itself to inscribe references to a deity on the dollar whilst simultaneously inserting such into the pledge of allegiance that children are forced to partake in at the beginning of every school day. Since then, many have convinced themselves that the United States is and always has been a "Christian nation" that was created exclusively for Christians. However, this twist in the West's history forever altered the once-cozy relationship between the public concern of policymaking and the private issue of one's religious beliefs. If the atheist is to be seen as an enemy of the state, then what version of a theist is to be hoisted up as a model citizen?

In the so-called Third World – to be identified here, collectively with the former "Second World", as the "East" for simplicity's sake -, the failure of secularism to catch on as it had in its industrialized counterpart is partially a side-effect of popular resentment towards imperialism; as perpetrated mostly by the West. While the former Soviet Union dabbled in their fair share of empire-building during the 20th Century, the empires of Great Britain, France, Spain, Portugal, and even the quasi-empire of the United States all cast a long shadow over the peoples of the affected regions. One generation after another in these societies experienced cultural suppression as the respective conquering nation demanded total obedience to a preferred way of life. Secularism, as a creation of intellectuals from these imperial powers, was nothing more than another piece of the oppressive puzzle.

When the Second World War ushered in sweeping changes wherein the empires of old were permitted to declare their independence, the age of empires left its cultural remnants and imperialism itself evolved. Instead of overt conquest, the developed world set out to convert the East by way of cultural infiltration and meddlesome military and diplomatic actions. Initially, this onslaught was waged

as an attempt to undercut the Soviet Union's potential influence – which, in turn,

was reciprocated by similar and less successful counteractions -, but the rise of

profit-driven globalization transformed the cultural clash into one of almost blatant

exploitation. Regardless of whatever humanitarian intentions the imperial

policymakers may have had, the consequences of their assault on the traditions of

disadvantaged people around the world – whether such was meant to fend off

"Communism" or to promote the interests of "Capitalism" – made the otherwise

commendable Western achievement of secularism an unacceptable tradeoff for the

way of life to which they had grown accustomed.

It should be stated candidly that the usefulness of attempting to separate

belief from policy – and vice versa - has expired. Among secularism's weaknesses

in the present is the current persistent perception of such as a Western philosophy.

Rajeev Bhargava (Bhargava, Rajeev, 2006) cites the rise of Iran's theocratic

republic in the 1979 revolution as an example of a "seismic tremor" dealt to the

"doctrine of…separation of state and religion". While the author notes the role

played by the uprising against colonialism's legacy in theocracy's emergence as a

popular option out "East", it is important to consider that religion instructs a

community's interaction with neighbors and enemies alike. It is also mentioned

that theocracy has been seriously considered by sizeable factions in other Eastern

societies of various religious beliefs (pg. 1).

Just as the West permeated the East with a cultural invasion before, the

East is now returning the proverbial favor as people move from one corner of the globe to the other and bring their beliefs with them. Bhargava (Bhargava, Rajeev, 2006) mentions the civil conflict being stoked by globalization as members of Earth's diverse faiths are flooding into and challenging the official and unofficial status quo. Not even the supposedly-secular societies have been immune from the tug-of-war as the dominant religious traditions thereof are forced to compete with the growing influence of "alien" viewpoints (pp. 1-2). True democracy is all-inclusive, and that means a secular democracy would have to treat the religious views of cultural invaders as equally legitimate. This is why secularism only works if religious views are not permitted to influence policies or if a society is religiously uniform.

In other words, secularism can not work in the real world; at least not without a degree of tyranny or anarchy. Secularism – a paper by Zachary Calo (Calo, Zachary, 2012) claims – tends to be more "exclusionary" by disregarding religion and what it means to individual members of the community. No, not all religious views are ignored, but those beliefs held by religious minorities are effectively outcast by society through policies molded by the believers enjoying a majority. As a result, "culture war[s]" – pitting religions against one another - become an inevitable consequence of having such a societal design (pp. 811-812).

Are such conflicts unavoidable? Given that faith in any particular doctrine is a matter of conscience, the truth is that no individual – whether they are elected or not – can remove their perspective on what life is all about from their participation in the democratic – or even undemocratic - process. In writing a law school paper on secularism and community, one Jeremy Waldron (Waldron,

Jeremy, 2010) underscored the necessity of having "convictions". He notes that an

individual's deeply-held beliefs are essential to informing their passion in dealing

with controversial issues "even if the…premises of these convictions

challenge…secularism" (pg. 1).

Another point Calo (Calo, Zachary, 2012) makes is that the dominant

religious views of the community which adopted a secular framework influences

how future generations will view the protections guaranteed thereby (pp. 812-

814). In this respect, "freedom of religion" gets interpreted to justify a narrow

guarantee for a select few. Additionally, the claim of "secular" government is even

abused as a cloak to suppress undesirable religions as being "illegitimate" and the

values promoted thereby as "untraditional". Here, it is obvious that the purported

intent of secular governance to safeguard religious liberty is nothing more than a

cowardly attempt to avoid genuine diversity and the important discussion that

needs to be had regarding justification for having such beliefs in the first place.

It may be important to point out that, contrary to remaining indifferent to

religion, two of America's founding fathers – James Madison and Benjamin

Franklin, as Nancy Glazener notes (Glazener, Nancy, 2008) – saw engaging

religion as the key to averting the tendency of civilization to tilt towards sectarian

factionalism. Of course, to them, the answer rested with promoting a pluralistic

framework so as to curb the danger of tyranny in the form of a faction becoming

too zealous and successfully seizing power. Essentially, Franklin was not a

believer that dispensing with religion overall was essential for devotion to reason

(pg. 221). Unfortunately, their vision is also unworkable in today's multicultural

America where political power doesn't exclusively belong to wealthy landowners whose beliefs were likely Christian in one way or another.

Rather than maintaining a position of indifference to religion, does it not seem more reasonable to gear government towards promoting a search for the truth? In a way, this could be seen as part of its role in the advancement of knowledge and in problem solving. As opposed to beginning this journey - to find the answers we've always yearned to know - with an absolute certitude such as proclaiming our state as Christian, Muslim, or Atheist, it would be far healthier to launch from a position of uncertainty. An Agnostic state is the only type of state which can honestly and equally seek to resolve the dilemma of blind faith, because it is the only approach which does not arrogantly claim to already know the truth.

Detractors will undoubtedly dismiss the advocates of an agnostic state religion as actually being "atheist". While many – or most – agnostics may be atheists at "heart", they at least remain intellectually open to the possibility that their personal conclusions may be proven wrong someday by way of observable evidence. On the other hand, there is some truth, and historical precedent, to the use of atheism as a pejorative. J.J.C. Smart once pointed out (Smart, J.J.C., 2011) that this term was more or less utilized by Romans to describe Christians – which was, itself, a term coined by the Romans as an insult – and others who rejected the pantheon of deities promoted by the empire (para. 2). So, while calling an agnostic or even an agnostic state advocate "atheist" may not be technically true as far as that person's position on the facts is concerned, he or she is technically an "atheist" as the Romans initially defined such given its rejection of the doctrinal status quo.

Likewise, the *Stanford Encyclopedia of Philosophy* article (Smart, J.J.C., 2011) highlighted the accepted origins of the term "agnosticism", having been derived from a philosopher named Huxley whilst partaking in a party. As it turns out, he was contemplating a more reasonable approach to the religion debate; one which recognized the improbability of ever discovering the universe's exact origins (para. 10). A better point – argued by a mathematician named Clifford, according to Smart – is that blind optimism irrespective of "the evidence before us" should be regarded as "morally reprehensible". Why? Reason being, that it compels us to ignore warning signs as well as our collective duty to take the proper course of action in accordance with reality (para. 12).

That's not to say that looking to and hoping for a brighter future is to be condemned, just that one should not ignore evidence in doing so. Clifford's assessment of optimism that dismisses the facts is less about being positive than it is about illogical faith. Humanity has a long history, as we've discussed here, of trusting in outcomes and myths even if they should know better. The goal of an Agnostic state is to remove this knack our species has for putting faith before the facts so as to clear a path for greater unity and realizing our full potential.

Until we reach that point, the arrogant declaration that we already know the truth is a non-starter for progress. Writing in an opinion piece for *Huffington Post*, Omar Baddar (Baddar, Omar, 2013) makes the case for agnosticism as the most intellectually honest position to take for the "open and skeptical minds" since it permits us to dispense with unjustified certitude and flatly admit that "[w]e don't

know" (paras. 1, 8). Part of his argument is based on humanity's currently limited

understanding of the cosmos and how it works at the "sub-atomic level".

Comparing our present intellect to that of a household cat's in comprehending how

appliances work, he explains that we still have a lot of evolving to do before we

could possibly uncover the mystery behind how our universe began (paras. 5, 8).

To clarify, this chapter is in no way promoting religious suppression,

unless one considers honest educational policies and pursuit of what science has to

offer as somehow subverting religious liberty. The Agnostic state is not a state of

oppression, but open-mindedness. If one is looking to exclude any viewpoint, then

they are not a sincere defender of democracy or even liberty, and exclusion is

precisely what agnosticism is designed to oppose. Ultimately, it is up to the

individual to determine – hopefully with more than just what they've been told by

family and friends - what he or she accepts as true, and nothing can change that.

Therein lays the basic reason why freedom of thought must always be preserved as

a foundational human right. With that, we prepare to explore the dual topics of our

freedoms and human rights

References:

Baddar, O. (2013, May 28). Why I'm Not an Atheist: The Case for Agnosticism.

Huffington Post on the Web. Retrieved July 4, 2014, from:

http://www.huffingtonpost.com/omar-baddar/why-im-not-an-atheist-the-

case-for-agnosticism_b_3345544.html

Bhargava, R. (2006). Political secularism. University of Victoria, Faculty of Law,

website. Retrieved July 3, 2014, from:

http://www.law.uvic.ca/demcon/victoria_colloquium/documents/Political

SecularismPreseminarReading.pdf

Calo, Z.R. (2012, October). Higher law secularism: religious symbols, contested

secularisms, and the limits of the establishment clause. *Chicago-Kent*

Law

Review, 87(3), 811-831. Retrieved July 2, 2014, from:

http://scholarship.kentlaw.iit.edu/cgi/viewcontent.cgi?article=3856&cont

ext=cklawreview

Glazener, N. (2008, June). Benjamin Franklin and the limits of secular civil

society.

American Literature, 80(2), 203-231. Duke University Press. Retrieved

July 1,

2014, from:

http://americanliterature.dukejournals.org/content/80/2/203.full.pdf

Smart, J.J.C. (2011, August 8). Atheism and Agnosticism. *Stanford Encyclopedia*

of

Philosophy. Stanford University website. Retrieved June 30, 2014, from:

http://plato.stanford.edu/entries/atheism-agnosticism/

Waldron, J. (2010). Secularism and the Limits of Community. *New York University*

Public Law and Legal Theory Working Papers. Paper 247. Retrieved July 2,

2014, from:

http://lsr.nellco.org/cgi/viewcontent.cgi?article=1250&context=nyu_plltw

p

Section Four: Human Rights

Chapter Eleven: Basic Freedoms and Rights

Chapter Eleven: Basic Freedoms and Rights

In philosophy, there is a debate about morals and ethics which focuses on absolutism and relativism. It can be said that the topic of human rights overall is one of morals. Is there any room for relativism whilst considering our rights? Does one culture or society have some morally superior justification for denying their citizens the rights enjoyed by people living elsewhere? Or are the rights taken for granted in societies such as the United States truly human rights to be absolutely guaranteed, without exception?

As we begin to explore the complexity of human rights, it is important to start with what many may consider the basics; at least for a civilized society. Humanity must ensure certain freedoms and rights in order for democracy to thrive, liberty to be genuine, and unity to be true and possible. Among these essentials are the rights: to dissent, to know, to have a reasonable expectation of privacy, and to due process in the event that one's freedom is ever in danger. In lieu of these, it is doubtful that anyone can ever sincerely be free.

Rights may be a relative notion to some, to those who prefer society to be guided by old traditions. What's problematic about leaving the designation of rights to out-dated societal designs is that the older the design, the more exclusive its nature. Absolutism – as far as rights and freedoms are concerned – is the only viable option for humanity. Regardless of how it would interfere with the time-tested standards of individual cultures, it is incumbent upon the human species as a whole to firmly establish and uphold these principles for all humankind.

Once we permit concessions on our collective rights in the interest of sensitivity to the reluctance of a particular society to modernize, we effectively reduce those same rights to nothing more than temporary privileges to be

whimsically given and taken away. A world where one's rights depend on the

willingness of local leading minds to welcome such with open arms is a

nightmarish one with no hope for the people to ever secure the reins. People

mustn't live in fear of retribution for disagreeing with the status quo, or for daring

to question popular thinking. By not universally guaranteeing these very basic

rights and freedoms, humanity is denying itself an opportunity to take the next big

leap in the evolution of our species.

First among these vital rights is the right of people to dissent. Writing for

CNN, Ed Husain (Husain, Ed, 2012) underscores the importance of the ability to

dissent in a democracy. Democratic governments must maintain a protection of the

people from repercussion for opposing the government in any way – except in

conspiring or making war against such – so that a tyrant or tyrannical regime

doesn't emerge with the deceptive veil of democratic support. In essence, fear of

the government is a hurdle which can't be tolerated if democracy is to survive

(paras. 1, 3-4, 13).

Not only should the right to disagree with the government be shielded,

but one's ability to oppose anything about the societal status quo ought to be as

well. It is crucial to bear in mind the fact that many societies are still led by

religious leaders or at least a certain doctrine of faith. In those places, it is often a

suicidal decision to explicitly take a stand. Your compatriots labeling you as a

"heretic" has a tendency to be far more dangerous for one's health than if the

chosen adjective were "traitor". Reason being, that heresy is seen as an affront to concerns of the soul, whereas a traitor is only turning his or her back on a creation of humankind.

Regardless of one's motivation to speak out and say "no", it is easy to overlook the necessity of safeguarding such. The right to dissent is the right to think independently. Disallowing the mind to work without artificial and arbitrary boundaries is a needless restriction on the wonderful and limitless power that free-thought provides. Permitting critique of the norm is how humanity fine-tunes our inventions, or conceives new inventions altogether, because it is the indispensible foundation of innovation and our continued collective progress.

Of course, free thought is useless in the absence of adequate information. Humanity ought to provide and secure the right to know, because informed decisions are akin to walking in a dark cave with a flashlight. For this reason, transparency in government and an emphasis on education are essential. Leaving the people to have no choice but to follow the leader is an invitation to chaos when the proverbial leader fails and the followers are left to fend for themselves. That's the type of thing that the worst revolutions are made of.

Realizing that you're getting a raw deal in society doesn't require an education or adequate information. Where the ability to know comes to play a role is in understanding why life is so horrible and in formulating a civil means by which to rectify same said injustice. In China – an article in *The Economist* shares ("Right to Know", 2014) – recent changes in law have enabled the citizenry to begin enjoying the benefits of some transparency. With the Chinese "version of a freedom of information [request]", a right granted in a law passed in 2008 to try and open the government up enough to stifle the continued rise in public

dissatisfaction with authority, citizens can seek answers to concerns they have –

which must be of "personal" importance – by either directly inquiring the agency

or requesting that the information be made available online (paras. 1-3, 6).

In the afore-referenced Chinese example of opening the government to

the public, a vital lesson can be extrapolated. Keep in mind that the people of

China are almost completely inoculated from the rest of the world. Despite not

having much interaction with the people beyond their borders, and despite the

government's success in cracking down on dissent, the powers that be have

determined that it is in their best interest to give the people some power in order to

curb the threat of upheaval. Just as with natural evolution, the evolution of society

– from tyranny towards democracy - can not be contained. Moreover, it is a good

idea to nurture that progress than to try and fight such by denying the people's

access to knowledge.

Although, it is imperative to note that the people don't need to know

everything. More specifically, the government – working on behalf of the people –

doesn't have to supervise everything that goes on in day to day life. While

transparency is a key component for holding others accountable – which is, in

turn, needed to make democracy work -, the privacy of individuals must be

protected. Honestly, this is about more than shielding a person from public

embarrassment.

Not that we should ignore the threat of making one's personal life a

circus show for all to see and scrutinize, because humanity has a terrible track record of exploiting mistakes and misunderstood behavior for entertainment's sake

as well as for political gain. In beginning their argument for the right to privacy –

or "the right to be let alone" -, Louis Brandeis and Samuel Warren explained

(Brandeis, Louis D., & Warren, Samuel D., 1890) how the protections of law had

evolved – from material concerns to the personal – up to the point in time at which

they composed their piece. Part of this attempt to express the importance of

privacy was in referencing the then-recent advent of "instantaneous photographs"

alongside the print media's growing habit of spreading gossip for the sake of

selling papers (paras. 1-5).

Furthermore, let's face it, if private matters are not regarded as sacred,

then oppression becomes easier. A tyrannical government need only take a peak

behind a dissenting citizen's closed doors to access potentially taboo details about

that person's life. In the event that such happens, same said government could

have leverage in compelling an influential voice of opposition to keep quiet. By

not erecting a resilient wall between the private and public realms, governance by

fear becomes more likely and democracy is rendered useless.

People mustn't only be safe from invasions of privacy to deter political

disagreement, but the safety of their conscience must be protected as well.

Expanding upon the essential nature of shielding privacy, the University of

Missouri-Kansas City's website mentions ("The Right of Privacy", n.d.) how a

United States Supreme Court ruling in 1969 pertinent to the then-controversial

issue of pornography saw the majority opinion convey why prohibiting against the

personal use – at home – thereof was a step too far. In penning the opinion, Justice

Thurgood Marshall said that the "State has no business telling a man…what books he may read or what films he may watch [...for it amounts to] giving government the power to control men's minds" (paras. 7-8). Our right to privacy is directly connected to our ability to think independently and make competent, reasoned, even critical decisions; no matter how popular or unpopular those decisions may be.

Just as vital as all the aforementioned rights is the right to due process of law. Here, the standard is that the government must ascertain that no one is deprived of their freedom unless he or she can be proven guilty of committing some act against the people. Protecting our freedom from unjust infringement is the final piece of the puzzle in this compilation of basic rights. A people must have confidence that their government can not arbitrarily lock them away – particularly for political or religious reasons -, or else the rights to dissent, to know, and to privacy become meaningless.

This 800 year old concept has stood the test of time, and has proven to be a major asset in reigning in the power of tyrants. Donald Wilkes highlights (Wilkes J.R., Donald E., 2006) the importance of due process in the evolution of society by pointing out that the protection was born with the Magna Carta of 1215 when the King of England was compelled to guarantee such. Over a hundred years later, parliament coined the term "due process of law" as a reference thereto. Remarkably, out of the many provisions of that historically important document, due process is nearly alone as one of the rights not since repealed in Great Britain (para. 3). This is no doubt a testimony to the indisputable necessity of making sure that the right in question is present.

While the British have preserved due process through statute, some are of the opinion that an official protection may prove to be a mistake. In America, the Framers – Erwin Chemerinsky (Chemerinsky, Erwin, 1987) writes – were concerned that an explicit guarantee of Habeas Corpus in the Constitution would enumerate a right that could later be taken away by the federal government. So, in the spirit of compromise, the right was implied via Constitutional prohibitions against the unwarranted suspension thereof. Furthermore, during Reconstruction, the federal government was granted greater authority in protecting one's right to be safe from unjust apprehension as a reaction to the South's overt attempts at preventing the former slaves from being free (pp. 752-753).

Whether or not our freedom is safeguarded via an explicit mandate, there must be an established recognition that we are free unless our own actions demand that society takes such away. The American Constitution's architects were rightly worried about compiling a list of rights, as an official declaration of what is protected could be interpreted to suggest that all others not included were somehow not worthy of protection. An argument can be made that it would seem more reasonable to make all rights implied and that only all things forbidden should be listed. In contemplating these questions, future human societies ought to ponder Thomas Jefferson's preference for each generation to rewrite their Constitution to fit the challenges and needs of their times.

So as not to drift too far away from the issue of shielding freedom from unjustly being denied or removed, it helps to enhance our understanding of what is meant by referencing due process and Habeas Corpus. Metaphorically speaking, Habeas Corpus is but a puzzle piece in the grander picture of due process. With that in mind, Habeas Corpus is the most important piece of that puzzle, as it represents a requirement of the government to resist the urge to be overzealous. This component of liberty must be included for any community to be genuinely civilized, even if a central government or policing authority is nonexistent. The accused mustn't fear a mob's irrational wrath, because the people have to realize that each of them - individually – is equally endangered when another's liberty can be easily dissolved for the sake of satisfying collective outrage.

If avoiding tyranny and promoting democracy is the objective, then those suspected of wrongdoing should always have an opportunity to confront and dispute the accusations levied at them. According to Cornell University Law School's website ("Habeas Corpus", n.d.), the main protection guaranteed by Habeas Corpus is the safeguard against unwarranted, "illegal detention". This is achieved by way of a petition requesting that the arresting authority or authorities present the "body" of the charges to justify the arrest or else be forced by the courts to release the prisoner in question (paras. 1-3). Ultimately, preserving this right requires that the entire process be transparent to enable the public's ability to hold the system to account.

Making these concepts universal – and absolute - is crucial to the success of a united, free, and ever-progressive humanity. Forgetting or excluding any of the basics risks creating distrust, which can later cause unrest and even conflict.

The people of the world must be empowered both collectively and individually for

a democracy – no matter the scale – to function as intended and to avoid a descent

into tyranny. While collectivism and individualism (two subjects to be discussed

more in a future chapter) may seem at odds, this chapter has helped underline how

the right of one to think freely and to dissent from the rest ensures that there will

be an unrestricted exchange of ideas. After all, it's this exchange which allows

humanity to continually fine-tune its inventions; including democracy itself.

Related to the rights of dissent, knowledge, privacy, and – to a smaller

extent – due process is the right of people to choose what's in their own best

interest. In the workforce, it does nobody any good to be compelled to take a job

that they dislike over one that they would be enthusiastic about. Arranged

marriages are equally deplorable since they remove the right of all participants to

select their spouse for more than mere financial or social convenience. Likewise,

forcing a woman or a family to give birth against their will is much more harmful

to society – and the affected parent or parents – than it is beneficial, and that will

be the topic at issue in the next chapter.

References:

Brandeis, L.D., & Warren, S.D. (1890, December 15). The right to privacy.

Harvard Law

Review, *IV*(5). Retrieved July 25, 2014, from:

http://groups.csail.mit.edu/mac/classes/6.805/articles/privacy/Privacy_bra

nd_warr2.html

Chemerinsky, E. (1987). Thinking about habeas corpus. *Case Western Reserve*

Law

Review, *37*, 748-793. Retrieved July 23, 2014, from:

http://scholarship.law.duke.edu/cgi/viewcontent.cgi?article=1667&contex

t=faculty_scholarship

HABEAS CORPUS. (n.d.). The Cornell University Law School website.

Retrieved July

22, 2014, from: http://www.law.cornell.edu/wex/habeas_corpus

Husain, E. (2012, September 14). Arab Spring nations don't yet grasp freedom of

dissent.

CNN on the web. Retrieved July 20, 2014, from:

http://www.cnn.com/2012/09/14/opinion/husain-arab-spring-democracy/

Right to know. (2014, May 3). *The Economist on the web*. Retrieved July 21,

2014, from:

http://www.economist.com/news/china/21601564-leaders-discover-some-

transparency-can-help-make-society-more-stable-right-know

The Right to Privacy. (n.d.). The University of Missouri-Kansas City, School of

Law

>   website. Retrieved July 25, 2014, from:

>   http://law2.umkc.edu/faculty/projects/ftrials/conlaw/rightofprivacy.html

Wilkes J.R., D.E. (2006) Human rights and due process of law. University of

Georgia

>   School of Law website. Retrieved July 24, 2014, from:

>   http://www.law.uga.edu/dwilkes_more/51human.html

The Pillars of Unitism
142

Section Four: Human Rights

Chapter Twelve: The Right to Choose (Abortion)

Chapter Twelve: The Right to Choose (Abortion)

Unity can never be a possibility in lieu of equality, and equality is nothing more than rhetorical if it isn't guaranteed for all; even members of both genders. For all of human history, most civilizations have regarded women as subordinate to men and important only when it comes to their role as wife, mother, and housekeeper. Serving man's every need – particularly his sexual desires – has been the woman's curse from one generation to the next. Regardless of her ambitious spirit, those dreams of achieving something greater than a household slave were condemned to a lifelong imprisonment detained within the body that she was so unfortunate to have at birth.

While slavery has existed in many forms and has affected populations throughout the world, no form of slavery has been as widespread and prolonged as the aforementioned servitude forced upon the female gender. It was only in the last century that women finally managed to gain even a modicum of respect for their contributions to humanity's progress or recognition of what they could potentially offer moving forward. For the woman, her primary obstacle is the popular perception that she is too frail or precious to do anything but procreate and nurture. This is probably the main reason that her right to choose when or if she devotes her body to birthing new humans has been met with such controversy. How dare she question the natural – or, more accurately, divinely-determined - order as we've come to see it?

Yet, questioning the status quo is precisely what women have been doing for much of the last century. The collective efforts of women fighting to break the proverbial glass ceiling may have only produced results for a fraction of women overall - even in the developed world -, but they have only begun to fight. This progress is important and should not be understated, as achieving change in societies with advanced democracies is an essential first step to realizing equality for all women in the future. Truth be told, tradition has been a steep obstacle to overcome.

Simply put, this is about power and the reluctance to share such. Men have – with few exceptions - dominated every aspect of human civilization, and have benefited from establishing the very norms which reinforce said dominance. For whatever reason, women were powerless when ancient scriptures and laws were conceived and inscribed, and they have paid a price for not being at the table during those crucial times. As has been the case throughout this book so far, the role of religion can not be ignored here.

Monotheism has a propensity for exalting men over women. When Judaism, Christianity, and Islam began to spread, myths such as Eve being a product of Adam's rib and ancient dictates about a woman's subservience overtook a number of polytheistic traditions with myths about heroines and goddesses. Moreover, those same pagan cultures were less adverse to women having some influence in society – including a number of whom who managed to attain power as Queens or Empresses -, but the Cultural Revolution which ushered in the so-called "Dark Ages" set women back for centuries. Tragically, not even the Enlightenment was able to break the man's grip of society's reins.

Despite the role that strong women had played in helping to promote and advance the era of revolutions - which effectively triggered the beginning of modern democracy's uprising -, equality remained a distant fantasy. In the United States, the Founding Fathers conveniently forgot the contributions of their wives, daughters, sisters, and other female compatriots in helping to secure their freedom, as women were completely excluded from the political process altogether. Fortunately, the women of America and the rest of the so-called "Western World" were not content to continue sitting idly by as the world rapidly changed around them. Throughout the Nineteenth Century, women developed a unified approach to addressing the social injustice of their exclusion, and they displayed a growing willingness to be civilly disobedient in order to elucidate such. By the century's turn, it was undeniable that there was no going back; men needed to give up their monopoly.

Women didn't just yearn for a say in the political arena, or greater economic opportunities, but were desperate to finally control their own lives. Before feminism gave her a voice, a woman's life wasn't a product of her independently-made choices. Chances are, if you were born with a uterus, your father, then your husband, and ultimately even your sons acted as your life directors. Men determined if and when you would marry, and to whom you would be married. They also chose when it was time to reproduce, and it was not uncommon for wives to be raped by their husbands to "fulfill their duties".

The rise of feminism was not simply about being bored with life at home, it was the natural – much delayed – consequence of centuries upon centuries of inter-gender oppression. To many, the abortion controversy represented the heart and soul of this struggle, since empowering a woman with the right to choose if and when she becomes a mother threatens man's strongest and most entangled

chains with which he is able to enslave her. Permitting a woman to have complete

control over her reproductive destiny is an affront to the traditional viewpoint that

she exists to bear and raise children, and it gives her authority over her sexuality.

This, not some concern over the fetus being aborted, is the root cause of abortion's

taboo status.

Honestly, if it were an issue of "life", then the opponents of abortion

should be the most militant proponents of social welfare programs aimed at

ensuring that all children are well-fed, housed, health-insured, and receive an

adequate education. Caring about the "sanctity of human life" shouldn't just be a

campaign slogan or a nifty bumper sticker to mask one's contempt for a woman's

independence from the dictates of a male-dominated society, but a cause to which

one is devoted at all stages of human existence. Of course, this is not the pattern of

political behavior observed with most policymakers – and perhaps even most

citizens - who proclaim loudly that they are "pro-life". Those same voices are far

too often missing in action when the focus shifts from "protecting" the unborn to

providing for the born.

All that anyone has to do to test this theory that the woman herself is the

target of anti-abortion policies is look at how passionately they fight against

abortion access for the unfortunate while turning a blind eye to services enjoyed

by the more affluent. The A.C.L.U. published a paper ("The Right to Choose",

2000) in which they discussed the American assault on the rights of poor and

teenage women to procure an abortion. In both cases, the aim of abortion's detractors has been to indirectly remove the option of terminating a pregnancy either through denying funds or via removing self-determination. This two-pronged assault on abortion's most disadvantaged beneficiaries coincides with a counterproductive onslaught against contraceptives, assistance programs, and tax benefits meant to ease the burden of bearing more children (pp. 2-3). If you truly treasure life, then you ought to look at how society can make the choice of introducing new life as appealing as possible. You can't opt to both restrict reproductive freedom and ignore the plight of impoverished families in the same breath without being perceived as hypocritical at best and oppressive at worst.

Yet, speaking out of both sides of their mouth is an art which has been mastered by the opponents of gender equality. It is likewise no mistake that many of them endorse policies which cut funding to education and/or underemphasize the importance of history. This is because the lessons that could be taught to the minds of tomorrow could help future generations understand that abortion – that is, abortions performed before a fetus is believed to be viable - has only been portrayed as a human rights issue in modern times. If we were to be honest with ourselves about this, the only rights related to abortion seriously debated in times past were the property rights of the unborn's father. So, by converting this moral dilemma into a battle over equality, the abortion debate was upgraded considerably.

Even so, that upgrade was slow to come. According to a paper published via New York University's website (Dionisio, Lisa et al, 2006), abortion has been in practice since ancient times; with controversy only emerging when "the father felt robbed of his heir". In early colonial America, a woman was permitted to get

an abortion until after 20 weeks of pregnancy, but the widespread exercise of this

right was largely kept in the dark due to the taboo topic of premarital intercourse.

All of this began to change during the 19th Century, when the American "medical

community" demanded that abortion primarily be restricted to a necessity

warranted by the mother's life being in peril (paras. 3-4). At each stage, the desires

and needs of the woman always came second to the interests and wishes of her

male masters.

Through a closer examination of how our ancient ancestors dealt with

abortion, you find that the only life which society claimed to worry about was that

of the mother. Make no mistake about it; her life was not seen as having the same

value as any man's, but abortion policies were designed to protect her life in

addition to the father's interests. The fetus – in "old Germanic", Roman, and

Jewish laws, according to M.J. Elsakkers (Elsakkers, M.J., 2010) – was considered

a part of the woman's body. In this respect, abortions were subject to punishment

as an affront against the woman. Where many of these prohibitions were

concerned, the so-called "poisons" supplied to provide a means of terminating a

pregnancy had to be regulated or forbidden altogether only because they were seen

as a health threat to the patient (p. 465).

It is tempting to think of this ancient concern for the woman's life as

proof that she had rights in society. Then again, her official status in much of the

civilized world at the time was barely above that of a common slave, and her life

was just as valuable – and expendable – as the man or woman who was forcefully bound to serve the family. Remember that a man was able to have numerous wives and concubines for the purpose of fulfilling his sexual and procreative needs just as he was empowered to own as many servants as he could afford. So, protecting the life of a mother was a matter of protecting the father's property, period.

The notion that abortion murders that which has yet to be born has undoubtedly been around for as long as has abortion. What hasn't always been a factor in the abortion debate until recently in human history has been the ability of this mindset to significantly curb access to abortion. If it is to be accepted that the opponents of abortion are truly uniform in purely looking out for the interests of unborn babies, then it can be helpful to consider how our ancestral leaders pondered this dilemma. Again, what you find in doing so is that the fetus itself wasn't the center of society's attention until recently.

Even during the era in which Christian theocracy was commonplace – the Middle Ages -, there was not some universal agreement holding that abortion was murder. Heather Webb wrote (Webb, Heather, 2011) – in reference to calls for prohibitions against post-heartbeat abortion – that Medieval beliefs about life's beginning included the notion that one's soul was not present until the brain was formed, and that a true "human" existence did not occur until then. Moreover, it is highlighted that humans "resemble tadpoles" in the fifth week of our development in the womb, with little more than a heart, a tail, and a circulatory system. In a more thought-provoking twist – with the tadpole image in mind -, Webb mentions how famed Christian philosopher Thomas Aquinas dismissed any beliefs that the

"Last Judgment" would feature embryonic souls rising to meet Christ, because – in

his assessment - they weren't really human when they perished (paras. 4-6, 8).

Looking further back into the mindset of humans in classical Greece, you

see – according to modern standards – a far more barbaric perspective.

Interestingly, Plato and Aristotle – as seen via the *Health Science Journal*

(Kourkouta, Lambrini et al, 2013) – were in favor of abortion's use as a means of

taming population growth. Plato actually went a little further, expressing a belief

that a society should abort all embryos belonging to women of an age beyond what

is deemed appropriate for breeding. As for limitations, with Aristotle, abortion was

unacceptable once the unborn reached "animal life" (p. 117). Appalling as these

views may be to contemporary humans; the simple truth is that earlier humans

were less concerned with distractive wedge issues than we are today.

If an aborted fetus really is a murdered human, shouldn't civilization have

been opposed to such from the beginning? How could our ancestors – who were

far more superstitious, on average – have missed the memo? What's apparent is

that the only constant in the history of abortions is that a woman has only recently

secured a hint of reproductive freedom. They are now more empowered to mold

their own destiny than ever before and the whole of humanity would do well to

expand upon – not rescind – this crucial right.

While some may be concerned with the father's claim to rights over

whether his offspring is born, Steven Hales (Hales, Steven D., 1996) shows how

the mother is able to justify having absolute ownership of her body and the

decisions about what happens to such. Perhaps the best point he implicitly makes –

whether intentional or not – is that a father can not have the right to deny an abortion, because he can not have the right to demand an abortion. Men can't get pregnant; therefore their rights do not extend to matters of the womb. With abortion, the greatest benefit that it offers is equality of self-determination, and even survival. Mr. Hales effectively underscores for his readers the importance of "choice" as far as circumventing "future duties" is concerned, but it is vital to remember that a woman may also be attempting to save her own life or even to spare her existing family a diminished quality of life (pp. 6-8).

Breaking free of the divisions which presently restrain humanity's potential must be achieved for unity to ever be realized. Unless women enjoy the same privileges as men – particularly when it comes to rearing a child -, there will always remain a great obstacle to our progress. Neil and Reva Siegel (Siegel, Neil S., & Siegel, Reva B., 2013) wrote – in a *UCLA Law Review Discourse* article – about how the United States Supreme Court has upheld a woman's right to choose as being a crucial matter that affects her "ability to control [her] reproductive [life]", which can ultimately determine whether she can ever be truly equal in society. In essence, arbitrary restrictions on this right serve no purpose other than to mandate the conservation and perpetuation of archaic stereotypes about gender roles (p. 165).

Why should society have a right to tell women what they can do with their own bodies? Is the woman somehow incapable of weighing the pros and cons of motherhood by her lonesome? As for the purported right of the father to have an offspring, what is it about him that gives him some special veto power over the woman's choice to endure a pregnancy? Is it not more humane or reasonable for a man to choose a mate with the same desires for procreation as himself? At what point does the woman actually have a right to self-determination?

Humankind must be egalitarian for unity to be possible. A woman must have the same rights and duties – that is, an obligation to contribute what one can to society - as a man. If she is denied equal recognition, then our species will never capitalize on its full potential. While it might seem hyperbolic to claim that abortion rights mark the centerpiece of gender equality, the reality is – as has been demonstrated here – that a person can only be as great as their circumstances permit, and one's destiny can never be bright if the choices which mold their life aren't theirs to make. In a related topic, opposing an individual's right to choose the terms and timing of their own death seems equally barbaric, and that's the topic we'll discuss next.

References:

Dionisio, L., Evans, C., O'Connell, P., Varshisky, A., Walter, W. (2006, February

28). A

Political, Public & Moral Look at Abortion. The New York University

website.

Retrieved August 9, 2014, from:

http://www.nyu.edu/classes/jackson/social.issues/papers/AbortGrl.html

Elsakkers, M.J., (2010). *Reading between the lines: Old Germanic and early*

Christian

views on abortion. University of Amsterdam website. Retrieved August

14, 2014,

from: http://dare.uva.nl/document/171177

Hales, S.D. (1996). Abortion and Fathers' Rights. *Biomedical Ethics Reviews:*

Reproduction, Technology, and Rights. Bloomsburg University of

Pennsylvania

website. Retrieved August 15, 2014, from:

http://departments.bloomu.edu/philosophy/pages/content/hales/articlepdf/

dadsrights.pdf

Kourkouta, L., Lavdaniti, M., & Zyga, S. (2013). Views of ancient people on

abortion.

Health Science Journal, 7(1), 116-118. Retrieved August 17, 2014, from:

http://www.hsj.gr/volume7/issue1/7112.pdf

Siegel, N.S., & Siegel, R.B. (2013). Equality Arguments for Abortion Rights.

UCLA Law

　Review Discourse, 60*, 160-170. Yale University, School of Law website.

　Retrieved August 18, 2014, from:

　http://www.law.yale.edu/documents/pdf/Faculty/EqualityFrontiers_REV

A.pdf

The Right to Choose: A Fundamental Liberty. (2000, Fall). *ACLU Position Paper*.

　American Civil Liberties Union website. Retrieved August 16, 2014,

from:

　https://www.aclu.org/files/FilesPDFs/ACF4E49.pdf

Webb, H. (2011, October 11). The Medieval Heart and the Abortion Debate.

Stanford

　University, Center for Medieval & Early Modern Studies website.

Retrieved

　August 13, 2014, from: http://cmems.stanford.edu/blog/medieval-heart-

　and-abortion-debate-0

Section Four: Human Rights

Chapter Thirteen: The Right to Die (Euthanasia)

Chapter Thirteen: The Right to Die (Euthanasia)

People have an understandable fear of dying. Likewise, our natural suspicions about policies which enable a physician or a loved one to assist someone in dying are equally understandable. Such fear stems from uncertainty, about what awaits us and the people we love after this physical existence, and about the frightening potential for abuse of a guaranteed right to pass away on one's own terms. While it may pain us to confess that death is inevitable, it can not be denied or ignored. Why then should we not be empowered to dictate when, where, and how we die?

To many opponents of euthanasia for humans, their position is that life is a gift given to us from on high. Taking your own life or taking the life of another is seen as a form of theft and/or rejection of this miraculous existence. Common support for the death penalty and war notwithstanding, their belief is that human life does not belong to us, thus it can't be intentionally ended. Our duty, in the "pro-life" viewpoint, is to wait for death to come. Besides, "God" or "the gods" only give you what you can handle, and everything which occurs was meant to be, right?

Destiny is the name of the proverbial game. Suicide, murder, abortion, and euthanasia are condemned for interrupting life, since each ostensibly defies the plan divinely written for the "victims". The irony is that if a particular deity were truly omniscient and capable of charting our life's path then an "untimely" or "premature" death can't really be in defiance of said plan. On the contrary, these taboo deaths have to be part of our fate, if such really exists. If not, then how can any serious person ever claim that "God" or "the gods" are all-knowing and all-powerful or that there is a thing called destiny to begin with?

Our fear of death is instinctual, but our irrationality about it is not. For that, we have religion to blame. Obedience to the status quo – of men and the divine - is often reinforced by promises of reward in the afterlife for our subservience. Rebellion, on the other hand, is threatened with either eternal torment or a permanent death of body and soul. While these primitive beliefs about death were understandable in the context of humanity's limited understanding of science at the time when they were initially conceived, it is no longer justifiable to continue perpetuating such willful ignorance and hysteria.

Far more logical is the reluctance to support euthanasia out of a fear to just let go. We humans have a propensity for attachment: to loved ones, to hobbies, and even to life itself. It is troubling to a great many of us that the people we care about want death more than life at a certain point. This disturbs us even further when we don't feel as though we are ready to live without the person seeking a merciful death. So, out of our selfishness, we wield what little control we do have over their existence to prolong life for as long as nature will allow.

Whether or not we aspire to do so; forcing a person to live when they don't want to is a form of torturing them. Empowering a human being to set the conditions of his or her own death is an achievement for which our species should be proud. Granted, we have not yet attained the ability to defy nature so as to live as long as we want, but we know how to make death painless, swift, and predictable. That is, if we want it to be. At the very least, we owe it to our suffering brothers, sisters, mothers, fathers, and others to give them the tools - that our advancements in medical science have provided – for ending life when, where, and how they want.

Equally repugnant is what the past of euthanasia-like practices have wrought for society. Whether it was for instilling fear in the masses or for settling old cultural scores, euthanasia has not always been merciful. Most obvious of the atrocious use of medically-induced or state-sanctioned deaths are the actions of Hitler's Nazi regime. Millions of people were exterminated as part of that horrid ethnic cleansing campaign and the world would do well to never forget such.

Of course, the Nazis were far from the first to murder their own citizens, but medical science made their goals easier to achieve. However, they weren't just trying to extinguish their perceived enemies from existence. Rather, the many victims of the Holocaust were oftentimes subjected to cruel medical experiments. This is usually the primary example of history which comes to mind when opponents or skeptics of euthanasia contemplate or debate the issue.

Society's current apprehensiveness on euthanasia also extends to their worries about how it would affect the weak. Human history tells a deplorable story about their treatment, and it would be naïve to assume that we've matured enough as a species to let down our proverbial guard. While the collective is capable of many wonderful things, the temptation to dispose of undesirables – particularly those citizens requiring a bit more assistance than others – successfully seduces our imaginations and influences our behavior from time to time. For this reason, vigilance in defense of the people who lack the ability to defend themselves can't

be extricated from any consideration of a merciful pathway to death.

There is a point, though, where such vigilance can become blind and even

produce results that are almost as cruel as euthanizing the needy out of a desire to

avoid tending to their needs. In an opinion published by the American Medical

Association back in the early 1990s ("Opinion 2.21 - Euthanasia", 1994. paras. 2-

4), the A.M.A. expressed that its opposition to euthanasia stems from a concern

that permitting such would endanger the helpless, "vulnerable populations", that it

would be "impossible to control", and that the best alternative would be to never

relent in guiding the dying to a peaceful ending. In theory, this seems to be

rational, as it is aimed at balancing the fear of suffering until death with the love of

life to which most of us still cling. The problem is, that the patient in question's

will is being ignored. They are not at peace for as long as they continue to live,

and every additional second that their life is forced to go on when the means exist

to extinguish it on their own terms is an additional second of torment imposed

upon them.

It is normal to view with suspicion any policies which may put the lives

of the frail in danger. As mentioned before, human history is riddled with example

after example of mass exterminations of weaker populations. In light of the

disturbing reality that genocide still occasionally rears its ugly head in less

advanced countries, we can't risk granting the right of a person to control their

death without keeping an eye out for those with ulterior motives. In a way, this is one of the few areas where the rights and interests of the individual trump the supposed best interests of the collective.

No matter how hard we try to eradicate selfishness, the individual or even an exhausted collective will forever remain tempted thereby. As has been underlined throughout this book, this is yet another reason why a strong, persistent educational system is essential. The importance of conveying the need for selfless compassion - via same said education - can never be overstated; especially when the rights to live and die are at issue. Whether the suffering individual is seen as a burden by his or her loved ones or by society as a whole, a person must never be intentionally stripped of their right to control their own fate.

What's truly puzzling is how long it took for humanity to begin the transition from leaving our deaths to chance to giving individuals a say. The Guardian notes (Guardian staff, 2014) that the first country to legalize "the right to die with dignity" was the Netherlands in 2002, and that the change in law came with strict requirements that the patient be suffering and near death with an "incurable" disease in addition to having "full consciousness" as to the decision being made (para. 1). No one can claim that such conditions are too loose or open to abuse. Furthermore, the need for a person seeking euthanasia to demonstrate that they comprehend the consequences of their choice ought to provide an added layer of safety.

Euthanasia's candidates need not fear an inhumane demise either. Perhaps one of the silver linings of humanity's experience in putting animals out of their misery is that such has taught us how best to extinguish life in as painless and swift a manner as possible. According to the article (Guardian staff, 2014), the Dutch provide this right via a "medically-induced coma" thus paving the way for the removal of "all nutrition and hydration" (para. 2). Is it not generally preferred to die in one's sleep? If an individual yearns to die at a time of their choosing, society has the means to – peacefully - accommodate him or her.

Difficult as it may be to accept, adult humans are not the only patients looking to end their pain. Time magazine reported (McDonald-Gibson, Charlotte, 2014) that – over the objections of people from within and without, including one plea from a toddler in Canada (para. 9) – Belgium became the first nation on Earth to extend euthanasia rights to children in 2014. However, this extended right to "die with dignity" comes attached with a strict set of terms which require the child to be competent about the choice he or she is making, near death with a terminal illness, and suffering devoid of any hope that medication can help. Furthermore, even after these hurdles have been crossed, the child would still have to be evaluated by doctors and other relevant professionals before getting parental consent for the "final decision" (paras. 1-3).

Undoubtedly, the very thought that a child would practically beg to die is heart-wrenching. Children are typically associated with an unbendable innocence, and civilized society tends to put their interests first as a result. Suffering, however, does not discriminate, and neither should mercy. With sufficient safeguards inhibiting a young person from being compelled to accept a premature death regardless of their will, humanity can comfortably offer the so-called "good death" to all; irrespective of age.

Since death remains mysterious – as far as what happens to our consciousness after life is concerned – and largely unpredictable when left up to nature, providing a degree of certainty when such is desired can make this inevitable part of our existence more tolerable. The human being is a species that has become accustomed to conquering nature and manipulating such to our benefit. In considering this reality, our current inability to avoid dying leaves a gaping hole that the scientific minds are sure to try and fill for as long as we are able to seek out a solution. In the meantime, we might have to settle for having the right to determine the conditions of our passing.

Euthanasia, quite simply, is humankind's best bet for solidifying control over our destiny. If living is the source of one's anguish, then it would be morally reprehensible for society to require that death be postponed any further. According to the B.B.C. ("What is Euthanasia?", n.d.), the term "euthanasia" is derived from a Greek word which translates into "easy death" (para. 4). Furthermore, it is underscored that most people seeking such an "easy death" aren't looking for pain-relief, but are suffering otherwise from an impaired quality of life and may be afflicted with issues of depression for any number of reasons; primarily their "dislike of being dependent" (paras. 16-18).

Another way of looking at this issue is through the lens of how euthanasia has been utilized before society began allowing humans to benefit from it. Do we humans not deserve the same degree of mercy that we extend to suffering nonhuman animals? Though many have a difficult time wrestling with the reality that we are – in fact – part of the broader animal kingdom, this is a question worthy of serious consideration. Why is it that we feel compelled to extinguish the life of a puppy in agony from an incurable ailment despite no clue that such is desired by same said puppy whilst recoiling at the thought of doing the same for a human when death is requested? Are nonhuman animals more deserving of mercy or are they less deserving of life?

Based on how euthanasia for these seemingly lesser life-forms is carried out, one would have to guess that mercy is the driving force behind such. Civilized veterinarians and medical students working with nonhuman animals take great care to ease their patients out of life, even when the animals in question are subjects used for experimentation. As an example, the University of Minnesota stipulates ("Euthanasia Guidelines", 2009) that their animals "[are] euthanized because they are experiencing pain or distress", and that the procedure itself is regarded as "pain-free or stress-free" (para. 1). Again, what entitles the nonhuman animals among us to more mercy than us?

Then again, mercy doesn't even have to be the primary concern for permitting access to human euthanasia. B.B.C. pointed out ("What is a good death?", n.d.) that many people fear not only a painful death, but a lonely death as well. Likewise, there is a common desire to say "farewell" to your loved ones before passing on. We humans yearn to control factors such as having our affairs in order before death, in addition to knowing – or even determining – the time and place of our demise. Granting us the "dignity and privacy" of an ideal death wherein our loved ones surround us – or not – empowers the need that many of us have to retain a hint of autonomy over our own fate (paras. 1-2, 4).

Having autonomous control over one's own life is a concept which can not be separated from democracy. At least, this is the case in our modern world comprised of humane methods to die before nature, accident, or an act of violence takes us. How can we claim "popular sovereignty" when the individual is prohibited by society to even die on their own terms? Is there something about euthanasia which contradicts the collective's interests?

Truth is, the collective benefits the most when individuals feel free both in life and death. There is no benefit to the whole in dictating whether an individual can choose to leave life. We possess the know-how and the tools to make life and death comfortable, easy, and obedient to our will. At the very least, it is incumbent upon us to grant our suffering brethren the right to die.

If we choose not to democratize death, then what is the point of democratizing life? Why even bother to permit any liberty when the most personal part of life – the end of it – is forbidden from our control? Life is not inevitable, but the end of any life lucky enough to live is. Restraining the will of any conscious being – providing that said will does not endanger the rights of others – is the ultimate unforgiveable sin and can not be tolerated in a true democracy.

The fear of death is overrated. While it may be terrifying to contemplate that your existence will one day cease, there is no detour from death. Likewise, to require that others remain prisoners of life because of your apprehensions about death or as part of your private religious beliefs is an infringement upon their liberty to live and die as they choose. For the sake of the collective, the individual's right to die must be protected and available to all. In the same spirit of this basic human right, we must now delve into another pertaining to one's quality

of life; the right to healthcare.

References:

Euthanasia Guidelines. (2009). University of Minnesota website. Retrieved September 6,

2014, from: http://www.ahc.umn.edu/rar/euthanasia.html

Guardian staff. (2014, July 17). Euthanasia and assisted suicide laws around the world.

The Guardian on the web. Retrieved September 4, 2014, from:

http://www.theguardian.com/society/2014/jul/17/euthanasia-assisted-
suicide-laws-world

McDonald-Gibson, C. (2014, February 13). Belgium Extends Euthanasia Law to Kids.

Time on the web. Retrieved September 3, 2014, from:

http://time.com/7565/belgium-euthanasia-law-children-assisted-suicide/

Opinion 2.21 – Euthanasia. (1994, June). The American Medical Association website.

Retrieved September 8, 2014, from: http://www.ama-
assn.org/ama/pub/physician-resources/medical-ethics/code-medical-
ethics/opinion221.page?

What is a good death? (n.d.). *BBC on the Web*. Retrieved September 9, 2014, from:

http://www.bbc.co.uk/ethics/euthanasia/overview/gooddeath.shtml

What is Euthanasia? (n.d.). *BBC on the Web*. Retrieved September 8, 2014, from:

http://www.bbc.co.uk/ethics/euthanasia/overview/introduction.shtml

Section Five: Economics

Chapter Fourteen: Healthcare

Chapter Fourteen: Healthcare

Is it humane to deny healthcare coverage? Should a society require that the collective or the individual provide insurance? Or, would the best course of action be to leave alone the decision to be covered? Many people view mandates for health insurance and/or universal coverage with suspicion in believing that such encroaches upon one's freedoms. However, it must be asked: are we truly free if we are left to suffer at the hands of medical injustice?

Moreover, how can freedom ever truly be claimed if a lack of adequate healthcare coverage increases the risk of public health dangers? Are civilized people not entitled to a reasonable expectation of good health? While you specifically may feel uncomfortable with a standard which ascertains that you will have access to medicine when necessary, the existence of such serves as a public safety net. In essence, health insurance isn't about you or me; it's about us.

In a primitive societal state, humans understandably utilized substandard means of catering to our physical and even mental needs. For the lucky few, this design presents no real challenge to maintaining a decent quality of life, since they likely have the right connections and enough disposable resources to both enjoy preventative care and pay for emergency needs. Everyone else is left to choose between one necessity and another, which is akin to making a decision about which limb is preferable to lose. The most nightmarish examples of anarchy-care involve the highly-superstitious wherein humans resort to pseudo-scientific remedies based on beliefs in potions, spells, and meditation.

While superstition may provide an individual with temporary psychological comfort, it fails to deal with the root cause of one's suffering. This

laissez-faire approach to insuring humanity with medical coverage is not only

irrational and inhumane, but it is also unsustainable. Forcing the poorest among us

to barter their possessions away for treatment of preventable illnesses harms

everyone in the long term for a number of reasons to be discussed in the coming

paragraphs. Should our species continue down this path of viewing healthcare as

the individual's concern or even as a relative cultural matter we will be hopeless to

prevent the global health crises to come.

In addition to leaving every human to fend for themselves, the profit

motive further degrades the mission of healthcare. From insurers to doctors,

having a private approach for an essential service such as maintaining public

health produces ill-conceived practices which only serve to increase profits instead

of working to guarantee a high quality of life. To provide an example, consider

that the often-praised Canadian healthcare system has one key problem which

remains intact – and which exists in the United States as well -: the ability of

doctors to boost their income by recommending and performing more surgeries

and other "unnecessary services", as a Harvard University paper by Elaine Bernard

mentions (Bernard, Elaine, n.d., pg. 4). For this reason, it is not recommended to

privatize any aspect of healthcare.

Society should avoid creating winners and losers wherever possible,

particularly when it comes to issues such as healthcare. Another important point

underscored by Bernard (Bernard, Elaine, n.d.) is that the Canadian "universal"

approach – as opposed to the American "targeted" approach – to social programs

such as healthcare coverage has been essential in maintaining unity of purpose.

Resentment, the author shows, is the product of a perspective holding that one

group gets special treatment over another. Moreover, the means-tested basis of

American social programs usually leaves the sole beneficiaries as those less

capable of lobbying for the strengthening or protection of those same programs

(pp. 6-7).

In truth, the path to covering everyone has never been easy. From the

beginning, controversy has followed this effort as the forces of individualism have

sought to undercut the objectives of universal coverage. According to the

Physicians for a National Health Program (Palmer, Karen S., 1999), a handful of

European states started this movement towards universal healthcare by providing a

mandate for "sickness insurance" in the early 1880s. From there, the rest of

Western Europe followed suit until shortly before World War One. Initially

envisioned "as a means of maintaining incomes and buying political allegiance",

this first step was seen as a compromise for the working people. Interestingly, the

conservatives in Great Britain and Germany offered this as a tool against the then-

rising tide of socialism (paras. 2-3).

Meanwhile, what was happening "across the pond"? In the United States,

the "talk" by Karen Palmer notes (Palmer, Karen S., 1999), the Progressive

movement largely hesitated to promote universal healthcare while the American

Medical Association actually once backed some compulsory coverage for the

impoverished. Then, when the First World War began and the pushback against all

things German – including their approach to healthcare – arose, the probability of

healthcare for all subsided. Compound that experience with the opposition of labor

– which feared socialized medicine hurting union power in providing benefits –
and the Red Scare, and you find the answer as to why the Progressive Era failed to
follow Europe's footsteps (paras. 4-5, 7-10, 12-13).

In the aftermath of World War Two, the reemergence of conservatism in
American politics and the second wave of anti-communist sentiments further
inhibited progress. Even the creation of Medicare and Medicaid weren't easy to
achieve as they were met with fierce opposition from the political and business
interests who most profit from capitalized care and who thrive from the hysteria
surrounding socialism. Though no politician would dare explicitly say that they
want to repeal these healthcare programs – particularly Medicare, given the
reliable strength of senior voters -, that hasn't stopped the conservative wing in
America from trying time and again to weaken such. Unfortunately, in the absence
of a strong leftwing alternative in American politics this persistent onslaught has
succeeded in framing a narrative that the social safety net is unsustainable and in
bad need of "reform".

Recently, the American healthcare system underwent a major
transformation which – from a broad perspective – gave the American people
more power in controlling their health. By forbidding health insurance practices
which limited or even prohibited undesirables from accessing coverage, the
Affordable Care Act – colloquially known as "Obamacare", initially as an aside
levied at the President who championed the reform and signed it into law – paved
a pathway to one form of universal coverage; that is, in theory. The bad news is
that this "reform" didn't address a slew of problems in the American system, and

ultimately left the root cause of its shortcomings – capitalism - intact. What the reformers refused to address and will eventually learn to regret taking on is the notion that healthcare is a commodity and that patients receiving care are consumers. This mindset must first be dispensed with in order to ever truly, adequately reform any society's healthcare system.

Depriving people - for any reason - of their natural right to seek out medical assistance when they need it is an unforgivable abuse. The precondition that a human must possess an individual means of payment in order to procure care is unconscionable when the whole of humanity collectively has the sufficient resources to care for everyone's needs. Thinking of medical care in terms of a product to be consumed is an epic mistake on par with charging victims of crimes for each time they contact the authorities to rescue them. If a person must have insurance to pay for their healthcare, then is it not equally valid to force every citizen to have "victims insurance"? Of course not, because protection from crime is an essential service as recognized by our human right to a reasonable expectation of security, and it is likewise just as absurd to require insurance in exchange for the essential service of healthcare.

By removing the so-called "middle man" in healthcare and having a system of direct coverage as paid via taxation, the populace is liberated to prosper and enjoy life. In arguing for universal health coverage, Kathy Lavidge of Yale University notes (Lavidge, Kathy, 2008) how the people of Great Britain are able to avoid the nightmare of having to display their health insurance card before getting care. Also, the people in countries with "single payer" programs don't have to fear an ambulance searching for a "charity" hospital as is the case in countries with uncovered citizens (para. 2). Additionally, the quality of life improves with universal coverage in part since workers wouldn't have to remain trapped in undesirable working conditions just for the abusive employer's insurance package (para. 4).

Are there shortfalls with universal coverage? Yes, but there isn't a single institution devoid of problems. The opponents of universal care are usually quick to jump at these errors such as the claim that people who live in countries with guaranteed insurance have to wait longer for "specialty care". While this is true – as an article found on Boston.com noted (Cohn, Jonathan, 2009) – it doesn't translate into avoiding care whether special or not, nor does it mean that these patients are ultimately left untreated or undertreated (para. 13).

On the contrary, to gloat about having a system lacking a guarantee of care just because it is easier for the lucky few with access to get speedy treatment is a failure of basic compassion. There is also the claim that an individualist approach to care produces better performance and results because of the supposed incentives for medical scientists to enrich themselves by constantly pursuing innovative means to address our health challenges. Related to these assertions, Mr. Cohn (Cohn, Jonathan, 2009) goes on to mention that the ostensible superiority of American care – pre-health reform – in dealing with cancer and other ailments is overhyped a bit. Reason being, that there are also a number of diseases and issues wherein the U.S. lagged and even some areas where the apparent supreme status was due to "idiosyncratic [- oftentimes excessive -] medical cultures" which had "nothing to do with insurance" (paras. 14-15). Besides, if a doctor has to be driven

by dreams of riches in order to develop something that could help humanity, then

they are not worthy of their sacred position.

Aside of the concern for the individual's well-being is the issue of how

the collective benefits from universal coverage. What's especially important –

other than public health, of course – is the strength of a society's workforce. A

workforce who is compelled to carry out their economic duties when their health

isn't at its best is not a very productive workforce in the end. For this reason,

universal coverage must also consist of a mandatory paid sick leave provision.

First and foremost, merely offering paid sick leave acts as a boost for

those employers who willingly do so. Perhaps they have done the math and

determined for themselves that it was actually cheaper to pay workers to stay

home when they're sick than to look for replacements. The absence of paid sick

days – a "fact sheet" from the National Partnership for Women & Families website

("Paid Sick Days: Good for Business, Good for Workers", 2012) shares –

produces an increase in costs and losses for businesses. On the one end,

"[turnover] can cost anywhere from 25 to 200 percent of annual compensation"

when factoring in the painstaking process of replacing employees. The other end

of this deals with monetary losses; which hurts an estimated "$160 billion

annually [for America's economy]" (pg. 1).

It doesn't take much thought to understand why a laborer would become

dissatisfied working under the employ of someone or some entity that doesn't

provide a compensated leave of absence in the event that nature calls your number to fall ill. Better yet, it should be a no-brainer as to why someone would be drawn

to work where such benefits do exist. Alec Arellano and George Awuor of the Bell

Policy Center shared a study (Arellano, Alec, & Awuor, George, 2011) wherein it

was found that providing paid sick leave improves productivity, reduces turnover,

and aids the affected society's public health while lowering the costs on its "health

care system" (pg. 1). A healthy and secure workforce is preferable to the

alternative, is it not?

By excluding compensated sick leave protections from any package of

universal health coverage, society effectively condemns the economy to a

perpetual state of unstable, sluggish growth. In elaborating on why sick leave is

important, the Bell Policy Center article (Arellano, Alec, & Awuor, George, 2011)

tells how workers lacking this benefit are left with the unenviable choice between

getting paid and getting better. Moreover, these laborers who work while sick are

slower to recover and threaten to spread their illness to coworkers and others (pg.

2). Isn't it madness to force the working person into a personally and even

societally dangerous dilemma of this nature? We either want the people to

collectively be at their best or we don't care about the collective's welfare at all.

Broadening the scope of humanity's mission to guarantee coverage for all

to include every living person on the planet will not be easy or cheap. Then again,

one can not seriously hope to unite all without including this essential protection.

People in the advanced parts of the world may belly ache about the costs of

taxation which accompanies the basic services, but these gripes pale in comparison

to the daily nightmare of living in the less fortunate parts of this planet. Would it not be better for us all to pool the world's resources so as to provide every citizen

of Earth with a guarantee of healthcare?

A report by the Center for Strategic & International Studies (Bristol,

Nellie, 2014) makes note of the troubling fact that roughly 150 million humans

suffer "financial catastrophe" each year thanks to a lack of affordable or universal

coverage. In narrowing this focus just a bit, Nellie Bristol tells of how the uprising

in Brazil demanding better care prompted their government to earmark a quarter of

the nation's oil royalties to pay for healthcare (pp. 1-2). Although – as the report

says – movements towards universal care have to be approached within the

cultural constructs of each individual society, the necessity for ensuring coverage

for all can't be ignored. The consequences could be dire for inaction ranging from

economic and political instability to dealing with the spread of dangerous

biological threats which could produce future pandemics if left unaddressed (pp.

4-6).

All the consequences for action and inaction aside, the people must

coalesce around a single, unified design. One thing that remains clear in the world

of universal coverage today is that the options for achieving coverage for all are

numerous. Again, we should remember that each individual healthcare structure

was built within the context of the local cultural framework. While humanity

would benefit the most from having a single approach for all, attaining this goal

must be permitted to happen organically, so as not to impede upon the precious

autonomy of any one nation or region.

T.R. Reid points out (Reid, T.R., 2008) that there are four models of health insurance, with the Beveridge Model – "[n]amed after [Britain's Health Insurance designer] William Beveridge" – providing that the people directly finance universal coverage via taxation alongside a predominantly, if not solely, government workforce providing care (paras. 2-4). The other three models include the so-called "Bismarck Model", the "National Insurance Model", and the "Out-of-Pocket Model". With the design crafted by Otto Von Bismarck of Prussia, insurance is covered by "employers and employees [via] payroll deduction", and the plans are required to be universal and nonprofit. In a "National Health Insurance" layout, private providers receive compensation from the government, and the laissez-faire "Out-of-Pocket" approach leaves every man, woman, and child to fend for themselves in a world where faith healers and bartering for care are considered as options on par with having adequate coverage (paras. 6-7, 9-10, 12-14).

The preferable option for pursuing a world with truly universal healthcare coverage would follow this pattern, depending on the starting design: transition from "out-of-pocket" to "national health insurance", then from "national health insurance" to the "Bismarck Model", and finally from the "Bismarck Model" to the "Beveridge Model". Each society should proceed incrementally so as not to cause significant disruption to their respective economic and political systems, and the end result should be a world unified by the so-called "Beveridge Model" wherein every healthcare worker from midwives and pharmacy technicians to physicians and surgeons would be public workers much like the police officer or fire fighter. Breaking free of the clutches of apprehension about ceding a degree of

independence for the greater good of all will be the biggest hurdle to overcome

here, but it can and must be done if we care about the whole of humankind.

Otherwise, we leave billions of our brothers and sisters to the whims of nature and

the luck of the draw.

A person's survival ought not to depend on their fortune or misfortune of

where and into what social status they were born. Furthermore, nobody should be

forced to choose between their health and their livelihood when taking a few days

off – with pay - would do no one any harm, but rather would likely improve the

worker's productivity and life satisfaction. Finally, it is immoral and unethical in a

world of abundant resources to profit off the needs of others, especially where said

needs can influence matters of life and death. While we strive to ensure that life

will be lived as healthy as humanly possible, our focus must also insist on

providing that a person doesn't have to work themselves to death in order to

survive. For that discussion, on the issue of guaranteeing that all may comfortably

retire in their "Golden Years", we head to the next chapter.

References:

Arellano, A., & Awuor, G. (2011, October 3). Costs and benefits of paid sick

leave:

reviewing the research. The Bell Policy Center website. Retrieved

October 7,

2014, from: https://bellpolicy.org/sites/default/files/PaidSickLeave_1.pdf

Bernard, E. (n.d.). The politics of Canada's health care system. Harvard

University,

School of Law website. Retrieved October 4, 2014, from:

http://www.law.harvard.edu/programs/lwp/healthc.pdf

Bristol, N. (2014, January). Global Action toward Universal Health Coverage.

Center for

Strategic & International Studies website. Retrieved October 1, 2014,

from:

http://csis.org/files/publication/140109_Bristol_GlobalActionUniversalH

ealth_Web.pdf

Cohn, J. (2009, July 5). Healthy examples. Boston.com website. Retrieved

September 30,

2014, from:

http://www.boston.com/bostonglobe/ideas/articles/2009/07/05/healthy_ex

amples_plenty_of_countries_get_healthcare_right/?page=full

Lavidge, K. (2008). Does universal healthcare make everyone's life better? The

Yale

School of Management website. Retrieved September 28, 2014, from:

http://insights.som.yale.edu/insights/does-universal-healthcare-make-everyones-life-better

Paid Sick Days: Good for Business, Good for Workers. (2012, August). National Partnership for Women & Families website. Retrieved October 8, 2014, from:

http://www.nationalpartnership.org/research-library/work-family/psd/paid-sick-days-good-for-business-and-workers.pdf

Palmer, K.S. (1999). A Brief History: Universal Health Care Efforts in the US. Physicians for a National Health Program website. Retrieved September 27, 2014, from: http://www.pnhp.org/facts/a-brief-history-universal-health-care-efforts-in-the-us

Reid, T.R. (2008, April 15). Health Care Systems – The Four Basic Models. PBS.org website. Retrieved September 29, 2014, from:

http://www.pbs.org/wgbh/pages/frontline/sickaroundtheworld/countries/models.html

Section Five: Economics

Chapter Fifteen: Retirement

Chapter Fifteen: Retirement

No living thing is equipped to labor until death. Even us humans, with our superior intellect compared to the rest of Earth's animal kingdom, have our physical limitations as to our endurance. Yes, there are many people who enjoy work and depend on it so much that they can't seem to live without it, but their resilience should not be extrapolated to suggest that all humans are capable of and/or should be compelled to do the same. At a point in most of our lives, it is incumbent upon society to ensure that we will have the right to retire.

Ascertaining the right to retire involves more than merely setting an age at which adult workers can leave the workforce, because there is no point to having an established standard for retirement if one can not do so comfortably. A comfortable retirement is one where a laborer's mind and body are allowed to be at ease and focus on matters which make the individual content. Having some semblance of hope that we won't be forced into endless work serves to relieve our conscience of any illusion of workforce oppression. So long as we have a reason to fear for the provision of our basic needs we will remain prisoners thereof, and freedom can not thrive under such conditions.

Of course, retirement hasn't always been a possibility - much less an option – for humanity. Then again, retirement wasn't always necessary. Our primitive ancestors not only lived shorter lives, but they worked less hard as well. It wasn't until the pursuit of profit was introduced into the human psyche that we started to force ourselves to work as if we were born to do nothing but.

Retiring in the pre-industrial world was a privilege enjoyed for the select few humans who managed to live past their 40s. Moreover, the market didn't demand that they overwork themselves whether or not the sun was up, year around, until the day that they collapsed. It was far from a perfect world, but our bodies were at least allowed to sufficiently rest between shifts; that is, unless you were in shackles, but that's another story. Now, with the accumulation of wealth driving our economic behavior, humanity is testing its resiliency like never before, and the need to ensure that a retirement will be possible has been placed front and center.

In capitalism, nature is instrumental, humankind is instrumental. Only wealth is perceived to have intrinsic value. Therefore, concern for the well-being of the laborer – much less their need to retire one day – is nonexistent devoid of the state acting on their behalf. In lieu of regulations protecting the right to have "golden years", a truly capitalist society would have no apprehensions about compelling the worker to exhaust themselves producing wealth until they dropped dead.

Capitalism is designed to accumulate wealth for the few, no matter the means to accomplish that end. For that reason, it recognizes no necessity for allowing humanity to rest. Instead, rest is seen as a hindrance to producing wealth since it results in lost time doing the bidding of the powers that be. When profit is the motivating force, only the callous and fortunate minority succeed and wind up secure enough to fully enjoy the pleasures of life as they grow old.

The safety net can not be created by a system built to serve the interests of ambitious individuals. Reason being, that an individualist approach to society emphasizes the strengths and weaknesses of each person and commands that one satisfies their desires and tends to their needs independently. The most that an

individualist-centered design is willing to offer as far as assistance is concerned is

charity; that is, a quasi-safety net which depends on the willful contributions of

other individuals. Since charity – also called voluntarism – relies on contributions,

its resources tend to be scarce with no guarantee of revenue.

Here is the reason that individualism – which produces capitalism - falls

short in ascertaining that people will have a guarantee of a secure retirement. We

can not expect to fully provide by leaving the existence of a safety net to

individual feel-good acts of "kindness" and to the presence of institutions created

for religious purposes or erected by a small group of compassionate humans.

When left to our own self-serving devices we all too often conveniently forget to

lend a helping hand. Preferably, humanity ought to employ the "veil of ignorance"

thought experiment envisioned by John Rawls.

Pretending that we are fully empowered to construct a societal approach

for the benefit of all equally without any knowledge as to what our social or class

status will be therein will allow any rational, fair person to conclude that all are

entitled to a reasonable expectation of rest after a life of contributing to society.

Quite to the contrary, a person is not inclined to agree – in lieu of the "veil" - that

his or her hard work should benefit another who is unable to contribute in like

fashion. This is why our awareness of sacrifice should be suspended for the sake

of contemplating the possibility that we too may require the assistance of society.

Again, uniting humanity behind a collective mutually-beneficial mindset instead

of a thought process which only focuses on how to enhance one's own materialistic worth is the only sure path to progress; including the protection of

humanity's right to stop working before death.

Remaining enslaved to the production of wealth for others is not how

humans should live out their days. Furthermore, depriving humanity of an

assurance that they won't have to die in the factory or at the desk is

unconscionable when the means exist to distribute resources in a manner that tends

to the essential needs of every living person. So long as the laborers have their

commitments to society reciprocated, there is no reason to doubt that they will

remain highly productive and satisfied up until the time comes for them to retire.

Prohibiting the hoarding of wealth and adopting a culture of collective duty can

not be avoided if a universal guarantee of retirement is the objective.

Uniting humankind under the banner of selflessness may appear to be a

radical concept, but it certainly isn't a new one. In discussing a book which

examines social safety nets around the world and which advocates for a universal

approach thereto, John Langmore (Langmore, John, 2014) highlights a basic

"principle of collaborative human life" featured in said book. The principle in

question suggests that any person whom believes that we humans have a duty as

our "brother's keeper" in terms of their "material welfare" ought to recognize that

we are obliged to guarantee a system wherein our fellow humans will at least have

their basic needs provided for them (paras. 3, 6). Here, as should be obvious via

the reference to an axiom derived from the myth of Cain and Abel, is an example

of how the foundational aspects of a united, collectivist model have been engrained in our thinking – though, not consistently applied in our interaction with one another - for many centuries.

The stronger and more broad the net, the more effective it will be at catching people before they plunge into helplessness. A comparison of the safety nets found in the American and Canadian systems in the 1980s by the National Bureau of Economic Research (Blank, Rebecca M., & Hanratty, Maria J., 1993) highlighted that poverty in the Canadian framework of universal coverage by the "net" was significantly less bothersome than what was found in the United States; with its predominantly "targeted" approach (pp. 197, 203). In essence, a society can't expect to eradicate poverty unless it is united, and there can't be unity when there is a perception that some are getting preferential treatment. Means-testing may sound good in theory, but it produces a mindset of "makers" and "takers" wherein the opponents of sacrificing for the good of all are easily able to make an argument against supporting the needs of the seemingly-"lazy" on the dole.

Either everyone should be promised protection by the net, or the net will be condemned to a constant recurring attack. People have to see that everyone has skin in the game and that the benefits will be enjoyed by all. Granted, some may be more in need than others from time to time, but the point is that no one ought to feel that they are exempted from contributing or receiving assistance when the time comes. This need to ensure universal coverage also requires a reexamination of values in terms of our individualistic love of self-enrichment.

Presently, the American social safety net has a weak guarantee of security. While it has proven effective at lifting millions out of deep poverty, the insufficient nature of its current design has rendered it insolvent and its

aforementioned effectiveness is depleting with every passing year. The reason why

it seems weak today is because the framers thereof never intended for it to be as

inclusive or expansive as it has since become, nor did they anticipate an economic

shift towards the service sector. In fact, the American model was originally

designed primarily for the benefit of so-called blue collar workers at a time when

well-paying manufacturing jobs represented a significant percentage of the

workforce.

The Social Security website tells us (Social Security, 2014) that the

American Social Security program "was never meant to be the only source of

income for [retirees since it only replaces] about 40 percent [of their income]."

Furthermore, it is stressed that a retiree is advised to secure "70 percent" of what

they earn regularly to maintain security (pg. 4). In theory, there's nothing wrong

with this design, but its success depends on a strong market wherein the

distribution of wealth is fair and constant. This is where the American approach to

a social safety net falls short, because its tendency to permit the wealthy to siphon

off the cash flow strangles the safety net in the long-term, thus resulting in a

gradual resurgence of deep poverty.

Over in Asia, though, we find a far more progressive model for the safety

net. In Mongolia – according to the International Labour Organization (Mongolian

Government Implementing Agency, 2010) -, one could retire after working and

paying into the insurance fund after 20 years once they reach age 60, though

women can retire five years earlier. Additionally, if you've raised four small children, a woman could seek retirement at 50 as long as they've worked 20 years. With respect to laborers subjected to varying degrees of "hazardous conditions", the retirement requirements are even less strict dependent on what your body had to endure (pg. 2).

In contemplating the example of Mongolia, it provokes the mind to wonder if their standard is the true appropriate measure for examining who needs to retire, and when. Instead of means-testing, would a conditions-testing not be preferable? Sure, it could be reasonable to require a general maximum retirement age of 65 or 67, but then exceptions could be made based on what the individual citizen contributed – regarding how hard they labored for the good of all – so as to allow an earlier full-retirement, if such is desired. Even the concept of factoring-in childrearing as an eligible job has its appeal, since it is no small task raising even a single member of the next generation. In fact, parenting a child – complete with life lessons, discipline, and etcetera – can be considered the most important role of any individual who chooses to produce offspring, given that the newborn will one day join the collective human family.

Another angle from which to consider retirement is the "why". That is, asking ourselves why humans want – or need – to retire. This is relevant and crucial to ponder since it influences the work and life satisfactory measurements. If society is sensitive to the legitimate retirement desires of its citizens, then it could be justified in expecting the citizens to contribute until the time comes to step away.

Whilst thinking about the rationale for retiring, we would do well to remember that laziness has very little to do therewith. John Bound and Timothy Waidmann (Bound, John, & Waidmann, Timothy, 2011), in submitting a working paper for the Urban Institute, discussed the reasons that some American seniors choose to collect partial Social Security before they are eligible for full benefits. They noted that people in their early 60s begin to apply for the disability benefits largely due to the income loss they start to experience as their health heads south (pp. 1, 4). It's not as if they are too lazy to work. Rather, nature is more powerful than the individual's will.

The debilitating affects of a life in labor notwithstanding, why do humans require a reason to retire? Moreover, why must we continue working tirelessly day in and day out as if our life depends on it? Is constant work even necessary? How did our species ever manage to survive before we worked all 24 hours of the day and every day of the week?

These questions make some uncomfortable as they challenge a culture of "hard work" which has convinced generations upon generations of developed world citizens that prosperity is the end-all, be-all of our existence. Contrary to what we've been taught to believe about our purpose, we are not born to spend every moment of life producing. Instead, the need to labor ought to be driven solely by profitless demand. That is to say, demand for a service to benefit the public as a whole. While retiring from any form of physical labor should be available for any and all laborers, the people should not have to wait until old age to enjoy the peaceful intervals of rest between periods of on-demand labor.

So, is it in our best interest to retire? Does having at least the option to stop laboring actually make a difference? Or is this need a mere figment of our imaginations, conjured up by years of frustration? One thing that is for certain is that the elitist would prefer that the working person continue working and stop asking such questions.

According to *Forbes* (Rubin, Rita, 2014), retiring could prove to be a boost to one's health…if they desire retirement. For those who yearn to escape the workforce, retirement could help make them healthier by freeing up time for the individual to focus on their needs; beyond paying the bills. One expert even noted that leaving the chains behind on your own terms "is comparable [- with respect to your health -] to reducing the risk of being diagnosed with diabetes by 25%". Again, the beneficial aspect of retirement is contingent on one's will. If they are forced to leave, then the health consequences could wind up being detrimental (paras. 2-3, 6, 14).

Knowing of the option to retire can provide the laborer with much psychological relief. There's nothing worse for the working person than the imprisoning thought of their toils being endless and pointless. The right to choose retirement empowers the worker with hope and makes for a happier, healthier, more productive, and wiser society in the long-term. Alternatively, hopelessness motivates nothing but resentment and plants the seed for revolution.

Change by force and onerous restrictions on progress equally inhibit humanity's potential. This is a constant truth in every facet of life, including the issue of retirement. When people are compelled to either retire or keep working against their will, then the inspiration of working for the common good is stripped

away. There is a better way than the approach which dictates strict terms of who

should work and how long they should work.

Rather than requiring retirement at a specific age, society would benefit

from a design which empowers the individual to gauge their ability to continue

contributing at the same level moving forward. If the laborer determines that he or

she is capable of staying put, then so be it. Ageism has no place in a united

society, for it arbitrarily reduces our productivity based on the assumption that

only the young are able. Otherwise, the next step – if early retirement is

considered or if a continued role working elsewhere in old age is desired - ought to

be taken after consulting others in the immediate community.

Should the elderly rest and play, volunteer and advise, or continue their

work as usual? Individuals should be given the benefit of the doubt in weighing

which path is best for them and society. Depending on the individualized

circumstances of working conditions, family, community, and etcetera, each

person will have a different set of factors influencing the course they take. In

cooperation with their community, the worker can pave a way forward once

they've had the time to sufficiently consider their options.

Much can be gained by ridding our collective conscience of the notion

that the oldest among us are helpless and must be forced out once they've visibly

grown gray and frail. Also burdensome is the belief that we must work until we

are incapable of normal function. Currently, the human family is divided by false

definitions of "hard work" and "laziness". We have been seduced for centuries by this myth of said labor being the pathway to useless, selfish, prosperity. In fact, the lust for riches has driven a wedge between us and has convinced the collective that it is better to work either until death or until the workforce deems you too pitiful to stay.

Retirement doesn't have to be this way. Instead of opening the door to the last stages of one's life, retiring can simply mean the ending of a single chapter thereof. Every human is useful to the whole for as long as society and the individual work together to make use of him or her. As long as neither the individual nor society makes a decision pertinent to retirement for purely selfish purposes, there can be no harm. Empowering the collective to control their destiny in the workforce is vital to the success of a united society. This is true of dealing with retirement, and it is especially the case when considering the role that social democracy has to play; the latter is what we'll discuss next.

References:

Blank, R.M., & Hanratty, M.J. (1993, January). Responding to Need: A Comparison of

Social Safety Nets in Canada and the United States. *Small Differences That*

Matter: Labor Markets and Income Maintenance in Canada and the United

States, 191-232. The National Bureau of Economic Research website. Retrieved

November 3, 2014, from: http://www.nber.org/chapters/c11149.pdf

Bound, J., & Waidmann, T. (2011, March). The Social Security Early Retirement Benefit

as a Safety Net. The Urban Institute website. Retrieved November 4, 2014, from:

http://www.urban.org/uploadedpdf/412313-social-security-early.pdf

Langmore, J. (2014, January 24). A social safety-net in each country: a necessary

condition for eradicating poverty? DevPolicyBlog website. Retrieved October 29,

2014, from: http://devpolicy.org/a-social-safety-net-in-each-country-a-

necessary-condition-for-eradicating-poverty-20140124/

Mongolian Government Implementing Agency. (2010, February 11). LAW ON

PENSIONS AND BENEFITS PROVIDED BY THE FUND OF SOCIAL

INSURANCE. International Labour Organization website. Retrieved November

12, 2014, from:

http://www.ilo.org/dyn/travail/docs/1704/Law%20on%20Pensions%20an

d%20Benefits%20provided%20by%20the%20Fund%20of%20Social%20

Insurance%201994%20-%20amended%201996%20-%20NATLex.pdf

Rubin, R. (2014, February 25). Retirement: It Just Might Be Good For Your Health.

Forbes on the web. Retrieved November 22, 2014, from:

http://www.forbes.com/sites/nextavenue/2014/02/25/retirement-it-just-

might-be-good-for-your-health/

Social Security. (2014). Understanding The Benefits. The Social Security Administration

website. Retrieved November 13, 2014, from:

http://www.socialsecurity.gov/pubs/EN-05-10024.pdf

Section Five: Economics

Chapter Sixteen: Social Democracy

Chapter Sixteen: Social Democracy

Organized labor is a feature of present-day life that we take for granted.

Why is that? How have we come to forget the contributions of labor unions to the

workforce, to our economy, and to our well-being overall? Is it possible that the

right to organize in the workplace has finally out-lived its usefulness, or is this

perception the result of a successful anti-union campaign that has been waged for

generations? When we contemplate these questions, we must do so both with a

firm grasp of labor's history and with a visionary eye towards what the future

holds.

In keeping with the theme of this book, the argument in this chapter will

be that social democracy – that is the concept of the people's collective power

determining our course of action in the workplace as well as in government – is

yet another essential piece of the pie to ensure the success of a united society.

Here, and in the next chapter, you will be asked to consider the strength of an

economy managed from the bottom-up, as opposed to the myopic, profit-

enhancing focus of the top-down approach seen in the "advanced" world today.

The laborer, in concert with his or her comrades, is better-equipped to discern the

best course of action in their work both in the short and long-term. Reason being,

that they are not detached from the consequences of their work either way, unlike

their corporate masters in the contemporary economic model.

Stretching as far back as – at least – the Middle Ages, this economic

hierarchy of wealthy master and peasant worker, with managers of wealth in

between, has existed in one form or another. Feudalism was the original design,

wherein the peasant would toil all his or her life to pay a perpetual debt to their lords. In essence, the peasant existed only to benefit the master. How has this relationship changed?

To be truthful, it hasn't changed a bit. We only ceased to call workers "peasants", our managers "lords", and our corporate masters "monarchs". The aristocracy never went away; it merely evolved by adapting to the changing sentiments of the people over whom it ruled. Present day feudalism masquerades as something called "capitalism"; which promises the supporters thereof that anyone with the drive to prosper can and will. In lieu of social democracy, the worst of this system is unmasked as the clever, greedy, and otherwise fortunate maximize their wealth at the expense of all.

While we may have deluded ourselves into believing the fantasy that the working person could one day rise to the top of the economic ladder if only they worked hard enough, the terrible truth is that the ladder we think we see is actually an obstacle course rigged – with unconquerable twists and turns - against social mobility. Those lucky few who do defy the odds do not prove the "dream" to be attainable. Rather, their unique stories are exploited by the system to further shame the suffering masses and provide an excuse for disregarding their needs. Nothing like a little discouragement to keep the hope at bay.

Consider the recurring battle over "minimum wage" standards. The fact that an employer – particularly a large one – has to be compelled to pay their laborers just enough to barely scrape by is telling of how they view the men and women who produce their wealth. There should be little doubt that they would pay their workers nothing if they could get away with it. Unfettered capitalism was built on the backs of slaves, and in some respects it still heavily relies on slavery.

Though explicit slavery is prohibited, this has not inhibited the greediest from treating the world's most desperate people as cattle. From the deplorable factories throughout the third world to the use and abuse of so-called undocumented immigrants in the "industrialized" world, the sins of slavery continue to plague humanity. In the United States, slavery didn't come to an end without a fight. Rather, it took the combination of a war and a dedicated movement of compassionate citizens to demand respect for the dignity of those humans being exploited for wealth and power. Today, slavery's demise must be connected to the interests of social democracy, for the fate of one laborer affects all others. This injustice will only come to an end in a globalized economy when the masses unite and demand an end to such.

With respect to the enslavement of minor laborers, children have been subjected to the harshest working conditions imaginable. While this nightmare may now be little more than historical fact in the "Western World", it is still an "in your face" part of life where most of the "West" gets their cheapest products. Often overlooked in the grand picture of exploited and "undocumented" labor is the role played by the young. If nothing else, are we not raising them to resent society or to feel that there is no purpose to life beyond the workplace?

Over a century ago, nations like the United States confronted this moral quandary. No, it wasn't that we suddenly awakened to the plight of young people. Instead, what happened was that laborers effectively organized, built their political power, and were able to convince the political institutions that some things have to matter more than profit. If it weren't for the unions of old, capital would still be the bottom line, and children in Southeast Asian sweatshops would not be so alien to us.

There is more to contemplate about a world devoid of organized labor. Consider, for instance, the lack of protections for working men, women, and children in Nineteenth Century America. Not only did one have to count on working most of every day, but they had to endure such in the most inhumane conditions. There were no restrictions on what an employer could make a laborer do. If the boss were so inclined, they could require you to carry a cardboard box of radiated items in your street clothes out in the boiling summer heat. The only thing which ultimately mattered was getting the job done, at any cost.

What the union does is remind the powers that be that humans are involved in making the product. Alone, no laborer stands a chance decrying the injustices of the workforce, but as one, working people demonstrate that they matter. When a union is formed and put to use, democracy is in action. Nothing serves as a more perfect example of the power of a people when they are united.

The importance of unions in balancing the interests of money and people is the primary reason why busting them has been a top priority for those who would rather not share the fruits of labor. Almost as soon as organized labor had peaked in its American economic power during the immediate postwar economic boom, the antiunion forces were working tirelessly to undermine them. In reality, there has never been a point when unions weren't faced with such fierce opposition, but the 1960s both marked labor's greatest strength and the beginning

of its steady decline. Starting with deindustrialization and outsourcing; the living

wage jobs which were represented so heavily by unions faded away as politicians

began to abandon their brief experiment with pro-labor rhetoric.

America's Middle Class, once the largest that the world has ever known,

has withered away. Crafty policymakers like Ronald Reagan proved effective at

convincing the people that unions were more a burden to society than a force for

economic justice. Now, the wealthy "job creators" aggrandize their riches by

selling worthless junk – manufactured by peasants forced to endure the inhumane

conditions outlawed long ago in the "Advanced" world - to the increasingly

impoverished public. Meanwhile, these same elitists promote a steady stream of

undocumented workers to labor in America's shadows by capitalizing on their

desperation so as to make yet another quick buck. Regarding the domestic

workforce, the trend is towards a permanent "temporary" or "part-time" design,

which benefits the short-term profit interests of the few at the expense of economic

security for the many.

It can be said that the greatest tragedy in at least American labor's

downfall is that the unions themselves have been successfully manipulated into

tolerating such. Instead of promoting economic justice for all, the powerful have

led the unions – or, more specifically, the membership thereof - to target the

exploited as the cause of their plight. They've become seduced by the myth that

the desperation of their suffering brethren – who work for next to nothing with no

organized effort to shield them - at home and abroad is speeding the decline of union representation when the real cause of their ills is greed...unbridled greed.

Only through solidarity, wherein the people stand up as one and refuse to

participate further in this oppressive system, can the exploitation come to an end.

For organized labor to function properly in any of its objectives, the

vitality of a united front can not be stressed enough. One way of looking at the

strength of labor unions is to compare it to a knight's armor. A single chink in the

armor could render the protective suit useless against a skilled opponent, and

disarray in the proletariat aids the interests of the powerful elites. Lest we

condemn ourselves to a perpetual state of servitude, the laborer must be prepared

to stand up for all laborers, not just the ones they prefer to call "comrades".

Additionally, unionization must be all-inclusive; leaving none to sit on

the sidelines. As Amy Dean explains (Dean, Amy B., 2014), participating in social

democracy – via labor unions – provides a collective benefit for the laborers. By

organizing, working people become effective at counter-balancing the intimidating

authority of their bosses (in a market economy), greatly increasing the likelihood

of having generous benefits. On the other hand, a system wherein a laborer is

permitted to enjoy the benefits of social democracy without contributing to the

cause creates long-term harm to all involved (paras. 2, 5, 8, 14).

In order to ascertain social democracy's maximum potential, the people

must see the connection between such and the quality of their lives. James Heskett,

writing for Harvard Business School (Heskett, James, 2005), conveyed that

organized labor must accentuate the individual's role in collective action as well as

the fact that everyone has something to gain or lose from such. Only then, the piece seems to suggest, can labor unions have a realistic chance at having a noticeable, positive impact in our global economy (paras. 2-3). There are no loners in the struggle for justice; we either prevail as one or ultimately fall due to our lack of unity.

Expanding on the individual's role, proponents of unionization ought to point out that each worker is responsible for one thing: participation. Participation in the workplace goes without saying, though it should be stressed that each person is expected to work their best. What is meant here is that all forms of democracy rely on active, persistent participation by the community. If the individual is apathetic, then that represents a failure of democracy, because he or she has not been adequately informed and/or inspired to safeguard their liberty. This is as true of democracy in the workplace as it is of democracy in society as a whole.

Devoid of social democracy, the worker is left to the whims of profit-based decisions. Typically, those in charge of making decisions geared towards profit maximization are focused on what lines their pockets in the short-term. When this becomes the case – without consideration for the immediate impacts on the working community -, labor exploitation is inevitable. Without a seat at the table, so to speak, workers can count on a reversion to explicit feudalism.

The question must be posed: should the worker have a say in their treatment? Contemplating this challenge ought to empower the laboring man or woman to see themselves as equally important as the men and women positioned as "supervisors". Ceding any ground to the supervisor class without a reasonable expectation of compromise in return is unacceptable. Overall, the arch of history

must bend towards decentralized power if freedom and shared prosperity are to be

desired, and de-unionization must be recognized as contrary thereto.

Empowering the worker is crucial to freedom and societal stability

because unbridled capitalism is marred by an insatiable hunger. The pure capitalist

does not concern themselves with the interests of society, much less the men and

women who work to produce the wealth enjoyed. Why should they when the

purpose of capitalism is…capital? In a system designed for wealth, by the wealthy,

the role played by humanity is to exist as property acquired by a hiring contract.

Capitalism is a beast which must be tamed, and the lion tamer is the

collective power of the people. Capital must be used to serve all, not to fill the

vaults of a few. It is useless in the long term for riches to be hoarded when such

can be kept in constant flux throughout a society. Here, organized labor can

ascertain that a society's resources are utilized to their maximum potential,

wasting nothing, for the betterment of all.

With unions in the mix, an economic system is kept honest by requiring

fairness lest a class struggle erupts. An article in *Time* (Liu, Eric, 2013) points out

how the mere presence of unions can have an overall positive effect on the

economy if the economic model is capitalist. A "strong" union presence lifts

wages for all – even the nonunion workers – through direct pressure on businesses

to pay the unionized more and "by creating a higher prevailing wage [for the

laborers not in a union]". When the presence is weaker, the oligarchy feels freer to hoard their wealth and with that comes less availability of jobs as well as greater

inequality (paras. 4-5).

A paper by the Economic Policy Institute (Mishel, Lawrence, & Walters,

Matthew, 2003) discussed some of the important contributions of unions. Among

the numerous benefits provided thereby is the safeguard of "workplace

protections". From advocacy for protection to educating workers of their rights

and even going as far as to monitor working conditions so as to ascertain

compliance, unions act as an employee's greatest ally in shielding them from

careless employers (paras. 39, 41). Considering just this information, it isn't hard

to imagine why the supervisor class thinks of unions as a nuisance.

Nuisance or not, organized labor polices the flow of a society's resources.

Well, at least it should, that is if the organization is strong and commands respect

from the supervisor class. There can be no certainty of economic justice devoid of

unions. Failing to decentralize economic power serves the interests of the few and

inspires their unbridled greed.

Democracy applied to economics is the only means by which to ascertain

a fair and equitable distribution of wealth. The people must have an opportunity to

offer their input into how their labor will be utilized and rewarded. A lax system of

nickel and diming the proletarian serves only to enhance the feeling of economic

oppression, thereby fueling a sentiment in favor of upheaval. If stability is desired,

then equality must be the goal of an economic model; and there is no pathway to

stability except through social democracy.

The supervisor class, however, - being puppets of the aspiring oligarchs –
are not content to cede even an inch to the working class. For a few generations,
their assault on the worker's right to organize has been relentless and has
succeeded in convincing many laborers that their organizational power is actually
a hindrance to their sharing in the great wealth which they help produce. A
confusing notion to the rational thinker, no doubt, but this twisted logic is
precisely why the elitists aim to weaken the worker's access to adequate
education. Dumbing down the proletariat is key to depriving them of their clout.

Workers are fed lies that trade unions will bully them this way or that,
and that organized labor has outlived its usefulness. They rely on fear and distrust
to inhibit any effort to unite colleagues, because they know that their counter-
arguments against a worker's right to organize fall flat when put against an honest
test of the facts. Stifling debate and demanding blind obedience is a staple of
oppression and we ought to condemn such in every aspect of our existence. It is
incumbent upon the working class to contest the amassing of oligarchic power at
our expense and on our collective backs!

Absent a solidly unified working class, the supervisor class has ferried us
to a new Gilded Age. Without a strong union presence in the economy or even in
politics, the people's interests have taken a back seat – if any at all – to the
insatiable hunger for the wealth and power of the few. Economic and political
decisions are made increasingly in accordance with whatever enhances the grip
that the oligarchs enjoy. Why has nothing been done? Blame the flow of

information, the success of "divide and conquer", and the influence of money in

politics.

Inequality is a natural result of a system designed to be subservient to the

affluent. As has been highlighted throughout this book, history holds a grim

prediction for a society so detached from the people. Our only hope is to recognize

the sin of concentrated wealth and restore the reins of power to the people. This

transformation commands all of us to participate, because sitting on the proverbial

sidelines is tantamount to betraying your rights as a human.

America's experience with social democracy has been a mixed bag. To

some, the American labor unions have done plenty, securing a broad swath of

labor protections throughout its history. For others, there have been many missed

opportunities. Which is it? Has labor lived up to its full potential when its power

was greatest? If one is to be honest with themselves then the answer should be a

resounding "no".

The power of the proletariat has been kept at bay by the supervisor class

and their allies in our "representative democracy" throwing the labor unions a

bone or two from time to time while also appealing to cultural squeamishness

about collectivism. This is done to ease societal tensions enough so that the calls

for overall reform subside, thereby permitting the status quo to remain unchanged.

In the United States, authors Quadagno and Harrington Meyer (Harrington Meyer,

Madonna, & Quadagno, Jill, 1989) underscored the argument by some that the

lackluster "welfare state" therein is a product of American labor's relative

weakness compared to their counterparts throughout the industrialized world.

While American unions certainly used social democracy to inspire changes to laws at each level of government – primarily by concentrating on the Democratic Party -, their culturally-ingrained suspicions about government intervention inhibited a full-fledged embrace of the revolutionary power exhibited elsewhere (pg. 182).

What the working class requires moving forward is an awakening. The worker must come to recognize that they are dehumanized by the current framework of global economics. He or she must learn how to work with their fellow oppressed by dispensing with the artificial labels which separate us. This struggle must be embraced across all borders, by men and women, to display an unyielding show of solidarity.

We, together, must resolve to transform our economic culture into one which meets the needs of all people. This can only be done by reviving social democracy and taking it to a level never before seen on a grand scale. Since we all have a stake in the health of our economy, it is best that all have a say – via organized labor – in how the economy functions. The resources that have been exploited by the elite for centuries do not belong to a few, but to all, and our economic behavior must reflect as much.

Moving forward towards a brighter, more united future, the proletariat must resolve to organize throughout the workforce. Not a single employee should be devoid of representation, as the lack thereof renders him or her helpless and vulnerable to an unaccountable hierarchy obedient only to the profit-motive. Laborers in every industry and field of work ought to form a union not only to fight for stronger rights and benefits in their particular job, but to prepare for a transition away from the supervisor-supervised framework. Ultimately, the goal should be to form an economic model for, of, and by the people.

Ideally, the objective should be to completely democratize the workplace. With the public owning the product and the workers producing such supervising one another mutually by way of their union, the hierarchy would be one of multiple levels of democracy as opposed to the present authoritarian model. Decentralized power at work and decentralized control of what motivates work is the best means by which to ascertain a just playing field. By maintaining the status quo of a few enriching themselves via labor exploitation we effectively guarantee that the injustice of deep recurring inequality will continue and only get worse over time.

For an example of a potential transitional model of ownership from the individual to the collective, look no further than one professional sports team in Green Bay. Jonathan Tjarks of Mic.com highlights (Tjarks, Jonathan, 2011) the importance of this team's ownership in reforming the sport of football overall. However, one could envision a bigger picture here as well. In Green Bay, the shares of ownership are spread out among thousands of fan-owners; in other words, the consumers own the product. No single shareholder is permitted to attain majority status and the team's profits are mostly earmarked for the good of the community. Despite their famously-small market size – especially when compared with other successful teams -, this team and their quasi-socialist model have done pretty well for themselves in recent years (paras. 2, 3, 5, 18, & 21).

Are we ready to take the reins? This question no doubt burns in the hearts and minds of serious revolutionaries throughout the globe. A better question, though, is: are we willing to keep tolerating life in the workforce as slaves of profit indefinitely until we are "ready"? At some point, the oppression must end and our societal evolutionary tilt towards enhanced democracy will overcome. The longer we wait to prepare for a transition to shared economic power the more in danger we are of a complete, violent, collapse of the system.

Forward we must go towards these unchartered lands. The people have never had the opportunity to work collectively for mutual benefit outside of what the motive of a few or even one demands. Through social democracy, our aspiring unity – which is crucial to the survival and advancement of our species – will be made possible as it promises to render the interests of greed obsolete by making sure that all enjoy the fruits of our labor. However, until we embrace the hard-to-swallow fact that capitalism can never be made to serve the whole, we will remain prisoners of selfishness thereby condemning us to an inevitable self-destruction. In the next chapter, our focus will be on using Marxism to understand how we got to where we are as well as our choices looking ahead.

References:

Dean, A.B. (2014, September 1). Free-riding on the labor movement. *Al Jazeera America*

    on the web. Retrieved January 3, 2015, from:

        http://america.aljazeera.com/opinions/2014/9/freeriding-on-

        thelabormovement.html

Harrington Meyer, M., & Quadagno, J. (1989, April). Organized labor, state structures,

    and social policy development: a case study of old age assistance in Ohio, 1916-

    1940*. Oxford Journals website. *Social Problems, 36*(2), 181-196. Retrieved

    January 7, 2015, from:

        http://socpro.oxfordjournals.org/content/socpro/36/2/181.full.pdf

Heskett, J. (2005, October 3). What's the Future of Globally Organized Labor? *Working*

    Knowledge. Harvard Business School website. Retrieved January 10, 2015, from:

        http://hbswk.hbs.edu/item/5029.html

Liu, E. (2013, January 29). Viewpoint: The Decline of Unions Is Your Problem Too.

    Time on the web. Retrieved January 8, 2015, from:

http://ideas.time.com/2013/01/29/viewpoint-why-the-decline-of-unions-

is-your-problem-too/

Mishel, L. & Walters, M. (2003, August 26). How unions help all workers. Economic

Policy Institute website. *Briefing Paper 143*. Retrieved January 4, 2015, from:

http://www.epi.org/publication/briefingpapers_bp143/

Tjarks, J. (2011, December 20). Green Bay Packers Prove That Public Ownership of

Organizations is Economical. Mic.com website. Retrieved January 14, 2015,

from: http://mic.com/articles/2952/green-bay-packers-prove-that-public-

ownership-of-organizations-is-economical

Section Five: Economics

Chapter Seventeen: Marxism

Chapter Seventeen: Marxism

Since the introduction of his theories – crafted and presented with the help of his co-author, Friedrich Engels -. Karl Marx has altered the course of human history in a way that can only be mirrored by the likes of Charles Darwin, Thomas Jefferson, or Isaac Newton (to name a few). Still, we in the Western World continue to lack a complete understanding of the world he saw and envisioned it becoming. Tragically, we wasted much of the Twentieth Century demonizing him and his work instead of attempting to learn more about it. What were we so afraid of?

Marxism is not some permission slip for tyranny, but this is a popular misconception that has been spoon fed to the advanced world since the Red Scare following the Russian Revolution. Was the call for revolutionary change as made by Marx exploited by tyrants? It most certainly was, but that is the case with any political theory or ideology. Do we not owe it to ourselves to explore further the points made within Marxism about the history and potential future of humankind's societal evolution? It's natural to be curious and it's dangerous – as well as, ironically, oppressive - to stifle such curiosity.

To fully understand Karl Marx's thinking, one must put such in context. In his time, true laissez-faire capitalism was nearing its peak and the explicit use of slavery in the "mainstream" was in its last throes. The rift between society's classes – the existence of which has always been denied by the powers that be – was precipitating a tremendous amount of tension which threatened to tear civilization apart. Men, women, and children were being made to work in the most inhumane conditions day after day with little or no protections, and those brave enough to organize with their fellow laborers were fighting – sometimes even

giving their lives – for a better work environment. In other words, Mr. Marx was

witnessing the worst that greed could produce for humanity in real time as

opposed to reading about it in some history book.

His vision wasn't that of some self-serving agitator, but that of a human

being who noticed a pattern in human history which aided in the enslavement of

humankind to the interests of property. Marx was not advocating – like Thomas

Hobbes before him – for a tyrannical system to rein in the masses. No, he was

promoting a future where the masses would be given the tools to break their chains

once and for all by coming together and marching forward as one. The future did

not and does not belong to some regime or an assortment thereof, but to the

collective. Unfortunately for Marx – and, arguably, all of us -, he did not live long

enough to see and defend against the perversion of his revolutionary theory and

ideology.

When the consequences of unbridled capitalism started to culminate in

the Twentieth Century's first two decades, exacerbating the tensions which led to

global war, the world was primed for a transformation. However, in a world where

the dissemination of information was still easily controlled, the elitists in the

Western World were mostly successful in taming an uprising of Marxist thought.

Meanwhile, the tortured history of less-developed states like Russia made a

people's revolt easier to achieve in a society lacking all of the tools essential to

making a safe, stable transition.

With the overthrow of Russia's monarchy in 1917 by Vladimir Lenin's Bolsheviks, the world was forever changed. By entering the First World War, the Tsar had sealed his fate – turning a great number of Russians against him -, but the revolution and bloody civil war which followed wound up harming Marxism more than advancing such. The images of violent societal upheaval and carnage gave the governments in the West an effective propaganda message to wage against Marx's vision; the Red Scare had begun. Up through the Great Depression, the people of the world continued to suffer from the growing disparity between rich and poor, but they were so frightened of abandoning the system which caused their suffering that they settled with sustaining such instead of pursuing a different course.

After a brief relaxation of Western paranoia about the "Communist" threat during the alliance forged in World War Two to defeat the fascists in Europe and the Japanese quest for empire, the tremendous display of fearsome might by the Soviet Union in crushing the Nazis and forcing the Japanese to surrender revived the Red Scare for a new generation. However, in the wake of a super destructive global war wherein an American superpower had emerged thanks to the obliteration of all other formidable economic and military competition, the only clear rival for dominance was the supposedly-communist Soviet Union. Since the economy had been rejuvenated by the massive amount of public dollars spent on mobilizing the country for war, the people of the West were finally feeling as if this "capitalist" system was working for them. A new, grand Middle Class developed thanks to the fallout of the war in addition to a number of other public investments. Meanwhile, the propaganda machine set its sights on "communism", because it would've been a shame for the Military Industrial Complex to be

dismantled to clear the way for peace.

The Cold War was not a product of a legitimate threat posed by the

Soviet Union. Yes, there were hardliners in Moscow who fantasized about global

domination, but the West never seriously considered coexistence a possibility.

Why? For one, an alternative option to what we called "capitalism" was not to be

tolerated by a weak democracy which had been hijacked by the wealthy few.

Secondly – and this is related to the first point -, choosing peaceful coexistence

meant that it would no longer be necessary for the people to pay – via their taxes –

for a select number of companies to manufacture tools of war. Abandoning the

profits to be gained by perpetuating a state of war was clearly not as appealing as

demobilizing and investing what was needed to transition to a prosperous era of

peace. Therefore, the fear campaign against the "Reds" was resuscitated so as to

create a mandate for retaining a portion of our war mobilization.

The tragically ironic part about all of this is that the supposed opponents

of "communism" were no longer defending a capitalist system. True capitalism

died with the Great Depression and has not been seen in the Western World ever

since. Rather, the taxpayers of the advanced economies have been conned into

subsidizing a war machine as well as the emergence of a service sector. Using the

American people as an example, we had been seduced into thinking that we were

fighting communism for the sake of defending our freedom and capitalism. In the

meantime, we were letting the elite chip away at those liberties, line their pockets,

send our brothers and sisters to die in needless wars for profit, and exploit our labor as we've transitioned from a capitalist state to a perverse welfare state where some tools of socialism are utilized to prop up the remnants of capitalism in order to ascertain that the few continue to accumulate wealth even as the rest of us continue to lose our share of the wealth produced.

Something else which should be considered is that the Soviet Union, Southeast Asia, Eastern Europe, Cuba, and China were never primed for a transition to communism. In order for a society to successfully evolve according to Marx's theory, its "superstructure" had to be advanced enough to avoid succumbing to tyranny or overwhelming its resources. The world's undeveloped or developing states lack the key characteristics required to make communism possible. In other words, the very societies which found themselves waging a "Cold War" against what they called "communism" were precisely the only states which could promote such.

Reason being, that the advanced capitalist states possessed the economic machinery – used for exploiting the many and their environment so as to enrich the few – as well as an accumulation of excessive goods which could be converted from a purely for-profit use to a public resource employed by and for the people. Additionally, the political structure and culture typically in place within said societies tends to give the people more power, even if said power is either rarely utilized or diluted by the unelected oligarchy's stranglehold over the elected. In the so-called "Third World", the populace is so accustomed to their oppression that being empowered via democracy is alien to them, thereby contributing to the chaos which typically erupts once an authoritarian figure or regime is toppled by a popular revolt. Without the proper cultural preparation, an exploited and repressed population will simply jump from one oppressive form to another; hence the reason why the experiment with Marxism in the aforementioned "communist" states failed miserably to produce the utopia Mr. Marx had in mind.

The reality that communism has yet to appear in human society does not prevent Marx's detractors from claiming that "communism failed". Nor do they seem to care that Vladimir Lenin, Josef Stalin, and Mao Zedong revised Marxism to fit their own political agendas. To the capitalist apologists, the rise and fall of Authoritarian – or Soviet-style – Socialism was sufficient evidence that Marx was wrong about there being hope for humanity beyond the individual-centric capitalist choice between anarchy and total oligarchic domination which awaits should we stay our current course. Never mind the fact that these same apologists gloss over the repeated failures of capitalism to save itself when inadequate regulation has led to hyper-concentrated wealth, thusly contributing to economic implosion. No, somehow Marx was wrong because of a handful of misguided experiments in less than a century, but capitalism gets approximately two and a half centuries to fail, get rescued by intervention, and fail again.

Before the West critiques Karl Marx, maybe we ought to learn more about him; instead of relying on capitalist propaganda. An article found at RT.com (Piskunov, Egor, n.d.) notes that Marxism hasn't been universally understood or practiced in the same way. For example, the Chinese "communists" – as led by Mao Zedong – turned against the Soviet Union's approach. To Mao, the Soviets had become too reliant on the methods of imperialists in order to achieve communism. From the bureaucracy to even the military structure, Mao saw flaws;

which he addressed by "praising…revolutionary youth groups and choosing

guerilla tactics as the only way to bring down imperialism" (para. 7). Despite

Chairman Mao's quasi-democratic thinking here, he and his regime failed to give

the Chinese people the reins of power, electing instead to retain top-down control.

Again, this is why the developed world, with an established – even if brief –

history of a mostly-healthy representative democracy, is where the revolution must

transpire.

Prior to embarking upon a different path, humanity has a responsibility to

understand the choices. Michael Burawoy, writing for the *American Sociological*

Review in 1990, discussed (Burawoy, Michael, 1990) the scientific aspect of

Marxism by first sharing the criticism by others about the very suggestion that

such is a science at all and then offering some arguments in favor of classifying

the theory as scientific. The criticism, for instance, stemmed – in part – from what

were perceived to be the "failed" predictions of Marxism; from "the absolute

impoverishment of the working class […,] the first socialist revolution [taking]

place in the [industrialized world…, and] that socialist society would be free of

revolutions". Pointing out that Marx offered "seven postulates" for what he called

"Historical Materialism" – a central part of Marxism's predictions about the rise

and fall of capitalism -, Burawoy insists that Marxism was not blinded by

ideology, but that the theory was molded by Marx's observations of humanity's

past and have been interpreted – for better or worse – by varying viewpoints from

the diverse set of "Marxisms". To Marx, the major factors for how materialism has dictated our past, present, and future were as follows (in summary): humanity has

to manipulate nature for their own benefit, society is defined and limited by the

means of our "mode of production", this "mode" is influenced both positively and

negatively by the choices we make in "how we produce" and determine the

"relations of production", when the disparity between the laborers and

beneficiaries of labor become too great a revolution becomes inevitable via class

struggle, a transition must be made possible with an available set of "material

conditions", humanity's forward movement is determined by our constant

emphasis on improving production, and communism represents the end of "social

antagonism" by way of allowing for collectively working to properly utilize the

very economic forces once exploited to our detriment. Perhaps the most

irresistibly haunting aspect of Marx's predictions is the role played by technology

in emboldening the greedy to maximize profits by cutting labor costs, thus forcing

"smaller" competitors to follow suit and eventually create a crisis of

overproduction where there "are more goods than can find consumers because

wages are so low" (pp. 778-781).

Biased observers tend to seek out reasons to discredit an idea at every

opportunity. With Marxism, the arguments against empowering the people to seize

collective control of their economy are influenced by the myopic critique of the

authoritarian regimes which supposedly pursued such and epically failed. It is not

unusual for these critics – whose loyalties lie with capitalism, not the people – to

disregard the cultural explanations for why communism never materialized to date.

For them, the cultural obstacles are a non-issue.

Then again, the West has to be educated as to what Marx and Engels

actually believed. Whether the detractors of Marxism want to acknowledge it or

not, the authors thereof most certainly saw culture as part of what traps a people in

their oppressive state. According to Douglas Kellner (Kellner, Douglas, n.d.) Marx

saw culture as part of the elitist "superstructure" designed – through the

emergence of "ideology" – to "cover over oppression, injustices, and [other]

negative aspects of a given society". Furthermore, since culture "appear[s]

natural", it is easy to disregard such when critiquing a society. Instead, many opt

to suggest that a society's culture – which may well be a contributing factor to its

failings overall – are beyond any extensive discussion about reform (pg. 1).

Culture, after all, produces and sustains the class system which entraps

and enslaves humanity. Our artificial notion of a societal hierarchy hinders the

human potential and serves the interests of a manipulative minority. Furthermore,

the status quo successfully safeguards their power by convincing the oppressed

that there is no class system – although, again, the classes only exist because the

oppressors desire such -, because one's status is all supposedly a matter of whether

one is responsible enough in their "hard work". Yes, if you are incapable of

escaping the lower class then it is because you failed in society as opposed to

society failing you. Realistically, the individual circumstantial fortune or

misfortune of birth has far more influence over where a person ends up in the class

system than does hard work or innovation.

R.J. Rummel once noted (Rummel, R.J., 1977) that Marx underlined

"three [major] classes [in] society: the bourgeoisie (who own the means of production…, and whose source of income is profit), landowners (whose income is rent), and the proletariat (who own their labor and sell it for a wage)" (para. 3). Therefore, as is clarified by the relations of classes to what they own and how such determines their income, "[one's c]lass…is determined by [one's] property. [Income and status do not establish an individual's class, but rather] are determined by distribution and consumption [of property]" (para. 4). In time, Marxism says, the natural progression of the capitalist society leads to a merger between the bourgeoisie and landowner classes. As a result, society sees wealth and power consolidated and concentrated into fewer hands, thereby pitting the elite against the many. Ultimately, the struggle over property distribution influences the distribution of political power once the proletariat becomes aware of their common status (paras. 6-7). Finally, this tug of war over power – via property – exposes the state as a tool of – and for protecting – the elite. Therefore, it becomes imperative for the people to overhaul the system by upending the bourgeoisie's grip thereof and beginning a transition to a classless, stateless society (paras. 8-9).

The elite manages to keep the masses on a leash by dehumanizing the laborer and rendering the fruits of his or her hard work meaningless for any objective other than to turn a profit. An article in the Library of Economics and Liberty website (Prychitko, David L., 2008) explores another aspect of Marxism; called "alienation". Here, Karl Marx is said to argue that the capitalist society's "anarchic" obedience to the pursuit of profit "blocks [humanity's] ability to take control of our individual and collective destinies". He felt that the enslavement of humanity to the profit motive stifled the masses from creatively developing a

"human society" by trapping us in a "degrading, monotonous, [machine-style

work routine]", and by "plac[ing] profitability above human need" (paras. 12-14).

The article's author (Prychitko, David L., 2008) also delved into Marx's

beliefs about the fate of "competition" under true capitalism. When left untamed –

or barely regulated – the market's progression towards expanded wealth for a few

will produce "a handful of monopolists controlling nearly all production"; thereby

"exploit[ing] workers and consumers alike". As for the so-called business cycles,

Marx predicted that the free market would prove to be unstable overtime "causing

huge swings in business activity […, including] severe economic depressions". In

the meantime, these swings – in conjunction with the monopolizing of economic

power – would give rise to "a greater supply of labor, a fall in wages, and…a

growing reserve army of the unemployed" (para. 18).

In trying to explain "alienation", Bertell Ollman (Ollman, Bertell, n.d.)

shows that Marx saw the laborer as having his labor not only separated from the

fruits thereof but also – sometimes intentionally – kept separate from his or her

comrades and the other basic features of normal life in the natural world;

particularly when it comes to "the distinctive potential for creativity and

community we all share [as humans]". As a consequence, our alienation – whether

by design or not – robs us the people of our power, and is self-replicated by our

consistent and obedient participation in the market (paras. 9-11). Permitting the

enslaved to think for themselves is the first mistake of an oppressive system, while

the second mistake is made when the masses are able to see themselves as a "mass". For this reason, suffering is individualized as opposed to being owned by the whole.

The curse of capitalism, the piece notes (Ollman, Bertell, n.d.), is that the never-ending struggle for more power – by the worker and the employer – leads the employer to constantly set out to undermine the attempts to organize labor and to maximize profits by relying more on machines and cheap labor. A corollary of this is that the market is left to rise and fall based on this selfish exchange of goods, thus producing repetitious economic crises as the workers produce far more than can be consumed due to a grand race to the bottom forcing all serious "competitors" to follow suit in exploiting labor for profit-sake. In the end, basic economics teaches us that the worker is also the consumer and that an insufficient compensation will not permit them to partake in the market. Therefore, their exploitation serves to condemn the market to self-cannibalization (paras. 16-17).

It should be obvious by now that under a capitalist system the lives of all are dictated by greed. Built out of the belief that empowering the individual with incentives to enrich him or herself will lift the whole of society into a state of collective prosperity, the end result has been an everlasting si-saw battle between wealthy competitors striving to overtake their economic adversaries at any and all costs. So long as there is something to gain via profit out of a particular act – no matter how insidious -, society can count on someone to exploit whatever has to be exploited in order to reap the benefits. Morals and ethics are of no concern when we are subservient to selfish indulgence.

On the other hand, what Marx offered was an alternative to a life directed by individualism. Though often misunderstood, the expression "dictatorship of the proletariat" is the rallying cry for the human species after many centuries of bowing to the will of money. No, this is not a plea for empowering some socialist dictator like Josef Stalin, but rather it is a promise that – should we choose the path of empowering the people – the oppressed will be oppressed no more because they will collectively and democratically control their destiny. In other words, the "dictatorship of the proletariat" will not be a traditionally-understood dictatorship wherein an authoritarian regime gives the populace commands, but rather a system where the masses no longer tolerate commands since they – yes, the people as a whole – would share political and economic power.

Such a system would be built not on the motivation of greed but on "need" instead. The exchange of goods would be out of necessity and mutually guaranteed through selfless acts of community-oriented duty to one another. Our moral and ethical concerns would likewise be better secured through such a design since upholding the same is in the collective's interests while defying said standards serves no one but the individual thinking of him or herself. By liberating the people from adhering to the whims of capital, the only dictates we require are those which nature bestows upon us for survival.

A century ago, the American economy was primed for a revolution. In the decades leading up to the Great Depression – especially during the age known as the "Roaring Twenties" – the economy kept growing, but the benefits thereof were being reaped by fewer and fewer people. Economic power was concentrated into the hands of society's elites, and the wealth gap between rich and poor reached

unbearable heights. When the system came tumbling down with the stock market

crash of 1929, capitalism was in real peril, and the people were given an

opportunity to abandon their class imprisonment in favor of a more equitable

design.

The people were starving and were tiring of the injustices plaguing their

existence. These injustices had become more apparent when the crash revealed just

how deep the disparity in resource distribution had become. Halfway around the

world, the Russian people had overthrown a tyrannical monarch in favor of a new

tyrannical regime masquerading as Marxist. Had it not been for the resulting Red

Scare, there's little question that the American working class would've given

Marx an in-depth look and that a revolution of either a violent or peaceful sort

would have transpired. Something was deeply wrong with our economy, and they

knew in their hearts that it wasn't working for the collective's benefit. It was clear

that something had to change.

Enter Franklin Delano Roosevelt and the New Deal, which effectively

saved capitalism from itself via selective, targeted socialist policies. By

establishing a minimum wage standard, guaranteeing some protections for the

workforce, creating Social Security, and employing those left without a job to

work for the public's benefit, the market was given a safety net both from

immediate collapse and from ideological defeat. When the Second World War

broke out and the country mobilized to wage such, the Depression was left in the

record books thanks to the boost in government spending which pumped a massive amount of money into the economy. After the war, the devastation of America's

trade rivals in Japan and Germany allowed – along with the built up economic

energy enjoyed by the people of America – the United States to dominate the

global economy and produce the world's largest-ever Middle Class.

Additionally, a mostly-progressive tax policy wherein the wealthiest

Americans were subjected to a top marginal rate exceeding 90% (on income raked

in after a high threshold, of course) was in place, and a Republican President –

with the support of certain corporate interests which had successfully dismantled

much of public transit to promote an individual-centered automobile culture -

pursued the construction of the great highway system. This redistribution of

wealth – occurring when organized labor enjoyed a peak in its membership and

power – helped to ensure that the people's resources would be utilized for the

benefit of the people, and kept the consequences of unfettered greed at bay.

Needless to say, the revolutionary conditions of the past were long forgotten as the

utilization of war and quasi-socialism helped prop up the once-endangered

capitalist system.

The hiatus of capitalism's worst characteristics was short-lived, however.

So long as the profit-motive exists in a political system where the influence of

money remains a factor, there will remain a few working tirelessly to reclaim their

throne. Greed is an insatiable monster which corrupts humanity in perpetuity, and

it requires a constant vigilance for society to cage this beast. When the Cold War

was peaking and the drumbeat for a war in Vietnam was growing louder, the

people's wealth began to shift back into those few hands once again.

Gradually, the unions started to lose their clout with deindustrialization and outsourcing as well as a prolonged campaign – as discussed in a previous chapter – to turn the people against their greatest weapon in the workforce. The capitalists changed the economic and domestic policy debate from one focused on maintaining "full employment" to one which emphasized the importance of taming "inflation". Tax cuts from the 1960s through to the early 2000s saw the wealthiest among us paying less and less as that burden was left to the strained and shrinking middle class. Raising the minimum wage standard has taken longer with each round over this same period of time, and the cost of running a successful bid for elective office has only skyrocketed. As a result, the representatives in our representative democracy are increasingly only representing the interests of the handful of people at the very "top" of our society.

If we are to be truly honest with ourselves, it would be inaccurate to describe the American political system as a "representative democracy" in its current state. The current distribution of political and economic power in America is more appropriately described as an "oligarchic-democracy". Yes, the people get to vote – though, not all of them have the right or even the desire to do so -, but their choices are pre-packaged by the warring factions of the powers that be. In essence, the elites present two slightly-different options in every election wherein the winning candidate tends to serve the will of America's oligarchy in varying degrees; depending on the political climate. No matter the electoral outcome, the top rung of society is always victorious.

So, what's the point of participating if our vote doesn't seem to make a difference? You see, that's exactly the point. The fact that you are even tempted to ask that question before bothering yourself to care about our political process is a testament to why we should care. In the end, your apathy and the apathy of our fellow oppressed is precisely what empowers the elites to begin with. When the people are deprived of their right – or will – to partake in our weak democracy, the weakness thereof is reinforced, exacerbated, and its ultimate demise is rendered inevitable.

Money in politics is a powerful and ostensibly insurmountable force in elective politics, but it is not impossible to overcome or eradicate. The establishment would like us to just accept that power rests in the hands of the few and forgo any fantasies of upending such. Reason being, that they know better than we that our vote and vigilant activism – should we ever attain class consciousness and mobilize to utilize our collective strength – are the greatest threats to their power. If liberation from our oppression is what we desire, then democratic engagement is the only answer.

Interestingly, this transfer of power from the people to the oligarchs wasn't a surprise to Mr. Marx. Michael Schuman, of *Time*, details (Schuman, Michael, 2013) how the modern emergence of global inequality could very well be fulfilling Karl Marx's predictions about the fate of capitalism. Even as capitalism seemed impervious to his predictions, the reality is that – as Marx said – the upper class's "accumulation of wealth" contributes to the working class's "accumulation of misery" (paras. 2-3). Absent some miraculous course reversal wherein the

wealthy holding the power suddenly feels charitable about their economic and
political dominance, the revolution draws nigh.

One major component of economics which demands our unified attention
is globalization. First, we must accept the inevitability of the world's economies
working as one. What doesn't have to be accepted as inevitable is the use of a
global economy to exploit the world's workers. Rather, the world's resources and
labor must be capitalized on – no pun intended – by employing the best that each
subset of humanity has to offer with their locally-available resources. For once,
globalization would become a tool for advancing humanity as a whole as opposed
to lining the pockets of the few.

Each culture could complement the others as the whole of humanity
works as one to ensure our collective survival. In some cases, it would be a matter
of transferring certain fuels or crops between regions or continents. Still, in other
cases, the technological advancements of this group could help support that group.
Yes, this is the basic nature of trade, but our species has never before done so for
the collective's welfare, alone.

Removing the profit motive from globalization is the key to guaranteeing
that humanity will prosper and attain a state of greatness that has only existed in
works of fiction. Globalized capitalism effectively imprisons our entire species
and binds the least-advantaged thereof to the whims of whatever turns a profit
most efficiently for the haves. On the other hand, globalized communism is the
only means by which – the accompanying political system notwithstanding – to
ascertain its successful implementation and longevity. This is because communism

depends on a pool of labor and resources that no isolated community could ever fully satisfy; it will either be all or nothing.

For us to succeed in uniting the human species and building an egalitarian, just world, there must be a transfer of power – preferably gradual – from the few to the whole. Decentralized economic and political power – the latter of which will be covered in our next chapter – protects all from the ambitions of a handful. This is because everyone involved in a collectivist society wherein power is not concentrated has a mutual interest to safeguard against tyranny, lest they fall subject to such themselves. In pursuing this transformation, we must consider that power exists as an illusion: those in charge are only at the helm because the people permit it to be so.

In the mainstream of western society any talk of abandoning capitalism continues to be taboo. We've been subjected to over a century of pro-capitalist propaganda which has only succeeded in maintaining the public's trust in the status quo because targeted socialism to help sustain such has been employed over that same period of time. Moving forward, the proletariat must be made aware of their common oppression and must be taught the importance of uniting - worldwide – as well as organizing to affect change. One caveat, though, as the revolution that must occur can not be successful if it follows the same path of the so-called socialist revolutions in Russia, China, or the like. Instead, we ought to resolve that this revolution be peaceful and all-inclusive; via democracy. Fortunately, our next chapter will delve into the equally-controversial subject of democracy and why this form of governance is so vital.

References:

Burawoy, M. (1990, December). Marxism as science: historical challenges and

theoretical growth. *American Sociological Review, 55*, 775-793.

University of

California, Berkeley website. Retrieved March 14, 2015, from:

http://burawoy.berkeley.edu/Marxism/Marxism%20As%20Science.pdf

Kellner, D. (n.d.). Cultural Marxism and Cultural Studies. Graduate School of

Education

& Information Studies, UCLA website. Retrieved March 16, 2015, from:

http://pages.gseis.ucla.edu/faculty/kellner/essays/culturalmarxism.pdf

Ollman, B. (n.d.). What is Marxism? A Bird's-Eye View. New York University

website.

Retrieved April 4, 2015, from:

http://www.nyu.edu/projects/ollman/docs/what_is_marxism.php

Piskunov, E. (n.d.). Marxism-Leninism. RT.com website. Retrieved March 28,

2015,

from: http://russiapedia.rt.com/of-russian-origin/marxism-leninism/

Prychitko, D.L. (2008). Marxism. The Library of Economic and Liberty website.

Retrieved March 27, 2015, from:

http://www.econlib.org/library/Enc/Marxism.html

Rummel, R.J. (1977). *Understanding Conflict and War: Volume 3: Conflict in*

Perspective. Beverly Hills, CA: Sage Publications. University of Hawaii

website.

Retrieved March 25, 2015, from:

https://www.hawaii.edu/powerkills/CIP.CHAP5.HTM

Schuman, M. (2013, March 25). Marx's Revenge: How Class Struggle Is Shaping

the

World. *Time on the web*. Retrieved March 23, 2015, from:

http://business.time.com/2013/03/25/marxs-revenge-how-class-struggle-

is-shaping-the-world/

Section Six: Politics

Chapter Eighteen: Democracy

Chapter Eighteen: Democracy

Of all the possible political systems to choose from, none unites the people and utilizes their collective potential better than democracy. Existing in various forms throughout history, democracy has always posed the greatest threat to elitist power. For that reason, the few have constantly attempted to restrain the influence of the many. Claiming over and over that empowering the masses would lead to selfish chaos and a breakdown of society, the power-hungry have managed to stall the next step of societal evolution towards shared political power.

Instead of a flourishing outbreak of democratic experiments the world over, we've been witness to a centuries-long struggle between fascism and the movement for liberty. Freedom can not exist separate from democracy, because it is only through decentralized power that we can ascertain such mutually. Dispense with whatever you've been taught regarding democracy being an unrealistic goal for humanity. Democracy is the future, this is inevitable, and it is up to us to facilitate its arrival on a global stage.

Peaceful, consensual democracy isn't merely the culmination of our evolution, but a factor in the existence of all intelligent species. Whether primitive or advanced, there is evidence which suggests that our prehistoric ancestors practiced democracy and that human beings aren't even the only species to employ this distribution of power. The implications of this information are that we don't need to concentrate power into the hands of a few to have order, and that disagreements don't require some all-powerful moderator to resolve. To say that a select group of elites are needed to lead us is little more than propaganda meant to stifle the many from realizing their potential.

A study published in *Science* (Morell, Virginia, 2015) found that democracy is more natural than we may have thought. For example, in decisions "affect[ing] the entire group", baboons will "vote with their feet". When only one or a minority of baboon "initiators" attempts to make a change, the others simply stay the course. This demonstration of "egalitarian rules" proves that conflict is not inevitable, nor is it preferable (para. 1).

Prior to classical Greece, humanity's experience with direct democracy may have been present for thousands of years. Evidence suggests – Robert Dahl shares (Dahl, Robert A., 2014b) – that democracy has existed since the days of hunter-gatherers. "Studies of nonliterate [tribes]" have affirmed as much, so long as they are truly independent from external interference. As it turns out, when humanity started settling and seeing massive population and wealth growth the spread of inequality produced an environment ripe for consolidated power in the hands of a few. Moreover, this power structure became reinforced by the eventual assumption – then myth – that rule over (not of) the many was "the most natural form of government" (paras. 1-3).

From these two important studies we see a key pattern; that democracy – not authoritarian rule – is the only natural political system. Before our ancestors were seduced by the quest for power in our increasingly-crowded social networks, consensus and mutual benefit guided our actions. Perhaps this is due to the fact that our "primitive" forefathers were closer in terms of intellectual progression to the other less-advanced members of this great animal kingdom. Maybe we just didn't "know better" than to be considerate of our brothers and sisters. Yes, democracy was working just fine until humanity learned to think selfishly and

resolved to design a society geared towards promoting the few.

When you learn about democracy through the approved curriculum of our

purportedly "advanced" educational system you are taught that democracy was

first experimented with by the classical Greeks of Athens. What the status quo is

really trying to say is that democracy only mattered when it was done by

"civilized" humans. Civilization is itself a loaded term since it designates all

groups of people outside of this narrow, "orderly" construct as being primitive.

Nothing ever accomplished by the subhuman – as perceived by the elitist mindset

– has counted for much of anything unless it is framed as a stepping stone to our

present greatness.

Still, there is much that we can learn from the Greeks. The *Ancient

History Encyclopedia* website describes (Cartwright, Mark, 2014) the first

historically-accepted democracy in Athens as "an extraordinary system…whereby

all male citizens had equal political rights, freedom of speech, and the ability to

participate directly in the political arena". These active participants weren't just

voters, but the servants of the institutions their actions created (para. 1). As part of

the Athenian democracy, the entire male population was empowered to partake in

their regular meetings, and the proceeds were presided over by nine presidents

who served "one time only" (para. 4). Interestingly, if the populace had come to

see any citizen as accumulating too much power, a secret ballot could be taken to

send him or her into exile (para. 5). Now that's what I call dedication to

decentralized power!

Contemporary critique of democracy is largely derived from the opinions of classical greats such as Aristotle and Plato. Yes, their perspective is valuable, since they were alive and witnessed this first-accepted experiment with the people employing direct rule. Additionally, the contributions in society's progress of minds of their ilk can not be dismissed. Having said all of that, we must consider the possibility that the disdain each man had for Athenian democracy is outdated.

For starters, let us examine Aristotle's worldview in context so as to determine if it should apply to the modern world. Fred Miller of the Stanford Encyclopedia of Philosophy highlights (Miller, Fred, 2011) Aristotle's viewpoints on what he deemed to be the appropriate and inappropriate forms of government. To him, political power had to be limited for the greater good, because the "city-state" existed to promote "the good life" consisting of "noble actions". Aristocracy – which literally translates to mean "power of the best persons" – was best for humanity in his view. Perhaps it is relevant to consider that he also felt that women were ill-equipped to lead and that owning slaves was in the best interests of the enslaved (paras. 15-19).

Remember also that Aristotle was Plato's pupil. While they seemingly disagreed on a range of different issues, it is instructive to consider the influence of Aristotle's teacher on his own viewpoint about how the world should work. These great Greek philosophers had at least one major thing in common: their trust in elitist power. Plato felt – according to Robert Dahl (Dahl, Robert A., 2014a) – that an aristocracy was the most appropriate governing approach with its "philosopher kings" (para. 8). Here you can see a key mindset against the people's power being established through the ostensible philosophical indoctrination of the

Western World's most celebrated classical mind.

In classical times, humanity was mostly illiterate. With that in mind it is

understandable why the dominant view of the day held that pure democracy was

not safe. To an extent, handing an uneducated and largely disengaged populace the

reins of power is comparable to giving a child a loaded automatic weapon. Once

the trigger is pulled, there's no telling what will happen.

For Plato – a piece in the *Neumann Business Review* reveals (Olepala,

Ogochukwu, 2009) -, democracy was dangerous because it empowered more than

the societal members whom "possess the principle portion of the soul that desires

for truth and wisdom". In his mind, the only citizens with this admirable quality

were the philosophers. Also interesting was Plato's apparent opposition to wealth,

given its tendency to corrupt humanity. Looking further into this classical

perspective, Plato and Aristotle were worried that greed would supplant the

general welfare as the driving force of a society ruled by the citizens. That's why

they felt more comfortable with political power left to a handful of select wise

men who would – in theory – be guided purely by the pursuit of justice.

The advocacy by Plato and Aristotle for aristocracy might have also been

rooted in what the former thought was the root of democracy: aristocracy's uglier

cousin, featuring the corrupted and abused empowerment of the privileged. Plato –

an author named Habib tells us (Habib, M.A. Rafey, 1998) – felt that democracy

was the natural reaction to the presence of an oligarchy. With an emphasis on

individual liberty and equality, democracy was believed to be the chaotic offspring of the deep inequality and oppression seen under the rule of a few. Furthermore,

Plato saw in democracy a lack of order, unity, or even a prioritization of education.

Since everyone was equal in a democratic society, everyone would naturally strive

to serve themselves as opposed to the greater good. This, his greatest fears held,

would inevitably produce tyranny (paras. 4-8).

In this respect, Plato and Aristotle were in good company with a leading

Framer of the United States. America's fourth president and chief architect of the

U.S. Constitution, James Madison, argued – in the *Daily Advertiser* (Madison,

James, 1787) – that the people could not be trusted to directly influence their

government since our greed would compel us to utilize "the first object of

government" – that is, protecting property – to enrich ourselves after uniting with

others sharing in our plight or affluence (paras. 6-8). This fear and rebuke of

"factions" in a democracy was the primary argument employed by Madison and

his ilk in the eighteenth century as they made their case for a federal union in

America. Basically, they were hesitant to support pure democracy for fear that

economics would inspire an uprising of the masses to confront the consolidation of

economic and political power in elitist hands.

Approximately two thousands years after Plato, his opposition to direct

rule by the people was influencing the molding of a new experiment with

democracy. The birth of the United States of America, with its emphasis on liberty

and popular sovereignty, is often hailed as a watershed moment in global politics

away from authoritarian rule and towards democracy. Yet, the model designed in

the 1780s for the governing of American affairs barely resembled a democratic approach at all. Instead, what the people got was a form of government that was largely aristocratic, with a dab of representative democracy in the formation of Congress. Then again, the supposed "representative democracy" was in and of itself intended to benefit the few since the only eligible voters initially were white, male, property owners.

Naturally, the American Founding Fathers were not unanimous in their distrust of democracy. An article in *Armstrong Undergraduate Journal of History* (Krause, Paul Joseph, 2015) notes that Thomas Jefferson wholeheartedly believed "that the common people could, and should, rule themselves independent of the directives of [society's elites]" (para. 2). His primary political adversary felt very differently about the distribution of political power. Alexander Hamilton, it turns out, was no fan of democracy, and trusted power more in the hands of the few (paras. 6-7). One may take note that the rivalry between them spawned the birth of political parties in the American political system, and this battle between their contrasting viewpoints persists to this day.

The modern Democratic Party evolved out of the Democratic-Republicans founded by President Jefferson. Where Jefferson diverges – according to Paul Krause (Krause, Paul Joseph, 2015) - with today's Democrats is in his distrust of a "larger federal government" for fear that it is too open to corruption by "big business and big capital". Instead, he felt that democracy was safer in the hands of "commoners", driven at a local level (para. 4). While the party has tended to stick to its roots of standing up for the common/working person, Jefferson's apprehensions about the clout of the elites have proven true even for the party which inherited much of his vision. In this respect, the influence

of money in politics – as well as the design of the American system - has played a

key role.

Moreover, the American political system was constructed with the

mindset that each elected representative would directly and solely serve the

interests of their respective constituents. In other words, they were intended to be

independent of national-based factions and loyal to the voters at home. Almost

immediately after the first president, George Washington, started to effect change

the resulting controversies over his policies gave rise to the very factions – in the

form of America's first political parties - that Framers like James Madison had

wanted us to avoid. Also interesting, Mr. Madison himself wound up joining the

more successful party of the original two-party system: the afore-referenced

Democratic-Republicans.

In theory, the layout conceived by the Founding Fathers was perfect; that

is, for a world where warring interests wouldn't organize to promote their cause.

Realistically, the greatest flaw of what they bestowed upon the American people is

that the model meant to elevate individual direct servants of the people in addition

to advancing each state's interests has instead produced a corrupt slew of partisan

loyalists, detached career politicians (in the worst sense of the word), and puppets

for the wealthy all packaged and preserved by an unaccountable two-party

dictatorship. So long as the current American political framework is maintained,

there will be no escape from the vicious cycle such creates. Only an awakening of the masses and a groundswell for reform – including a constitutional amendment

or two - will upend the present order in favor of an approach which best serves all.

A study published by the National Bureau of Economic Research

(Persson, Torsten, 2005) found that parliamentary democracies prove to be more

beneficial to the public's economic interests than do presidential systems.

Additionally, the comparative strength of the parliamentary approach is enhanced

when it is designed as proportional as opposed to majoritarian. Reason being, that

a proportional parliamentary system fosters a culture of consensus, which results

in policy-making serving the interests, needs, and even desires of overwhelming

majorities. On the contrary, a majoritarian presidential system leans on adversarial

politics which creates gridlock and slows progress (pp. 7-8).

In order to make democracy work for everyone, humanity must come to

terms with what works for the collective and what doesn't. For instance, pitting

two or more factions of citizens against one another works only to forward the

interests of a few, whereas pursuing an area of common agreement between

groups which disagree can instill a sense of community where each participant

feels that they've gained and sacrificed some for the common good. For us to take

that leap into a truly democratic model, we have to clear the greatest hurdle for

democracy: entrenched conflict. One assumption of democracy – as pointed out by

Jane Mansbridge in 1984 (Mansbridge, Jane, 1984) – is "that [the] citizens'

interests are in constant conflict [, thereby giving rise to adversarial democracy]"

(para. 7).

On the opposite end of the democratic spectrum, Mansbridge (Mansbridge, Jane, 1984) alludes to cooperative or "consensual democracy" which fosters inclusiveness and equality with the underlying belief that there is a "common interest" (para. 8). The *Governance* article further illustrates that the original, pure form of democracy's emphasis on equality produced an economic system balanced for all. However, as society shifted towards a more individualist focus, the democracies formed within those contexts produced the self-centered economic design accompanied by the perpetually conflict-ridden political superstructure found in the West today. In summary, the assumption that the people must always be in conflict over power accompanied by an every man for himself economy has left modern democracy in a state of disunion and an uncertain future (paras. 11, 16-19).

Listening to the naysayers – whose bias towards elitist power is obvious -, you would come to think that only representative democracy is possible. Digging even deeper into their mindset, the preferred approach of the proponents of concentrated power is one which discourages unity and which exploits the divisions within a society. Yes, this perversion may – for a time – work to benefit the few, but it sews the seeds of societal collapse. Without cooperation, a people cease to see their destinies as intertwined, thusly preventing them from desiring a consensus.

While the American-led West likes to claim that it produced and has advanced modern democracy, the West hasn't done anywhere near enough to nurture the rise of legitimate democratic rule. Contrary to the popular myth propagated by the West about the best forms of democracy, an article in the

European Journal of Political Research points out (Schmidt, Manfred G., 2002)

that the non-majoritarian, "negotiation democracy" – or one based on consensus –

produces the best outcomes in terms of "protection of minorities, voter turnout,

[and] income inequality". Additionally, studies show better rates for these more

inclusive democracies when it comes to benefits for the people as well as "energy

efficiency[,...] lower incarceration rates[,...] generally less punitive regimes, [and]

higher levels of satisfaction with democracy". Unity of society is likewise made

easier to come by when emphasizing the "majority rule" isn't important, because

the dissenting viewpoint is integrated (pp. 148-150).

Matt Leighninger tells us (Leighninger, Matt, 2006) – in his book about

the evolution of democracy – that active citizen participation throughout the

political process is key to improving turnout and the outcome. As part of this

argument, he describes an inspiring tale of a community in Rhode Island wherein a

local group of activists display the power of community unity to solve problems

and in helping to make their government more effective. In their case, the

challenge was cleaning up the town by fighting drug dealers, graffiti, and even

prostitution in concert with their elected officials. Alone, any citizen would be

relatively out-matched, but together they can't be stopped (pp. 25-31).

A people divided in a perpetual power-grab between factions make little

progress in the long-term. Of course, no one is always going to agree with their

compatriots, but to promote a system which intentionally facilitates an atmosphere

of conflict is to ensure that a society will ultimately fail in providing even basic needs. Unity is the best remedy for any challenge - regardless of its scope -,

because the input of one great mind can be compared with that of another and

eventually improved upon as a result. That, in essence, is the very spirit of

democracy.

Beginning the transition to a global democracy is imperative and perhaps

even inevitable as part of humanity's societal evolution. Additionally, as we

embark upon this empowerment of the masses, it is essential that our

understanding of democracy and all that it entails is as complete as possible.

Otherwise, building and expanding the people's power will be tantamount to

arming a group of children with deadly weapons. When taking on the political

options of humankind the people ought to explore which economic systems best fit

with each respective political system. In the next chapter, we will examine the

accompaniment theory: a theory that asserts every political framework must be

accompanied by a particular economic design in order to function appropriately.

References:

Cartwright, M. (2014, October 13). Athenian Democracy. Ancient History

Encyclopedia

    website. Retrieved June 14, 2015, from:

    http://www.ancient.eu/Athenian_Democracy/

Dahl, R.A. (2014a, November 4). Democracy. Encyclopaedia Britannica website.

    Retrieved June 18, 2015, from:

http://www.britannica.com/topic/democracy

Dahl, R.A. (2014b, November 4). Democracy: Prehistoric forms of democracy.

    Encyclopaedia Britannica website. Retrieved June 20, 2015, from:

    http://www.britannica.com/topic/democracy/Prehistoric-forms-of-

democracy

Habib, M.A.R. (1998, July 14). Identity and Difference: Plato and Aristotle on

    Democracy. Rutgers University website. Retrieved July 1, 2015, from:

    http://habib.camden.rutgers.edu/talks/plato-and-aristotle/

Krause, P.J. (2015, April). Claiming Thomas Jefferson: The Jeffersonian and

    Hamiltonian Genesis of American Progressivism. *Armstrong*

Undergraduate

    Journal of History, 5(1). Retrieved July 17, 2015, from:

    http://www.armstrong.edu/Initiatives/history_journal/history_journal_clai

    ming_thomas_jefferson_the_jeffersonian_and_hamiltonian

Leighninger, M. (2006). *The Next Form of Democracy: How Expert Rule is Giving*

Way

to Shared Governance… and Why Politics Will Never Be the Same.

Vanderbilt

University Press; Nashville. Retrieved July 10, 2015, from:

https://books.google.com/books?id=m_ZF8JZydPQC&pg=PA252&lpg=

PA252&dq=form+of+democracy&source=bl&ots=A7fTsRVqlR&sig=kS

C70PbeaZOeGFDVJcDHDEFgnKQ&hl=en&sa=X&ei=wgdhVcS0JIKw

yATO8YHgBA&ved=0CDcQ6AEwBDhQ#v=onepage&q&f=false

Madison, J. (1787, November 22). The Federalist No. 10. *Daily Advertiser*.

Constitution.org website. Retrieved July 21, 2015, from:

http://www.constitution.org/fed/federa10.htm

Mansbridge, J. (1984, Autumn). Unitary & Adversary: The two forms of

democracy. *In*

Context, 7, pg. 10. Retrieved July 11, 2015, from:

http://www.context.org/iclib/ic07/mansbrdg/

Miller, F. (2011, January 26). Aristotle's Political Theory. Stanford Encyclopedia

of

Philosophy website. Retrieved June 13, 2015, from:

http://plato.stanford.edu/entries/aristotle-politics/

Morell, V. (2015, June 18). Signs of democracy seen in typically authoritarian

baboon

society. *Science on the web*. Retrieved July 15, 2015, from:

http://news.sciencemag.org/evolution/2015/06/signs-democracy-seen-

typically-authoritarian-baboon-society?utm_source=facebook&utm_medium=social&utm_campaign=fa

cebook

Okpala, O. (2009, Spring). Plato's Republic Versus Modern Democracy. *The*

Neumann

      Business Review. Neumann College website. Retrieved June 28, 2015,

from:

      https://www.neumann.edu/academics/divisions/business/journal/review09

      /okpala.pdf

Persson, T. (2005, March). Forms of democracy, policy, and economic

development.

      NBER Working Paper Series, Working Paper 11171. National Bureau of

      Economic Research website. Retrieved June 21, 2015, from:

      http://www.nber.org/papers/w11171.pdf

Schmidt, M.G. (2002). Political performance and types of democracy: findings

from

      comparative studies. *European Journal of Political Research, 41,* 147-

163.

      Harvard University website. Retrieved June 29, 2015, from:

      http://www.hks.harvard.edu/fs/pnorris/Acrobat/stm103%20articles/schmi

      dt_Types_of_demo_and_perf.pdf

Section Six: Politics

Chapter Nineteen: The Accompaniment Theory

Chapter Nineteen: The Accompaniment Theory

Theories are a complicated part of human existence. While it is easy to conjure one up, the true test of a theory is putting it into practice. With economic and political theories, the trick is finding the right combination, because attempting to partner an incompatible group of political and economic visions will lead to chaos and inevitable failure. For that reason, this chapter is aimed at delving into what is itself called the "Accompaniment Theory".

What is the Accompaniment Theory? This is the belief that one must accompany any political system with an economic system that empowers the same group in order to ascertain its success. For instance, if a political system emphasizes the power of the people, than so to should its accompanying economic system. Furthermore, to avoid confusion and an unintentional mismatch, there should be an explicit determination of whether this framework is individualist or collective in spirit.

As was explored in the preceding chapters pertinent to democracy and Marxism, the economic model of communism and the political model of democracy are both dependent on the collective power of the governed. So, would it not make sense that these two models ought to be paired in order to guarantee their mutual success? Is there any sufficient evidence to demonstrate that communism can survive without democracy or vice versa?

The Accompaniment Theory can also apply to other economic and political models. Corporatocracy can not exist or function without an oligarchy, a monarchy is dependent on feudalism, and capitalism is best fitted for a society in anarchy. Regardless, the theory teaches us that the natural course of humanity is towards a shared destiny where the masses are empowered. No matter where a

society begins on the spectrum, the progressive evolution of civilization is in the

direction of collectivism.

Concentrated power is contrary to the interests of humanity, and it is

inconsistent with democracy. The people can not thrive if they have to bow to the

will of a dictator, whether politically or economically. In the Western World, it is

customary to accept that capitalism and democracy are compatible and that neither

can exist without the other. Truth is that the two models empower the masses and

motivate action for different reasons.

When there is a mismatch of the economic and political models, the

system slides into disorder. For this reason, two of the dominant models in the

postwar era have failed: the capitalist-polity and the socialist-autocracy. The latter

largely collapsed first and we are presently witnessing the downfall of the

capitalist abomination which has infected the globe with its blind pursuit of riches

and false promises of equality. What about this set of combinations makes them so

unstable?

Let's start with the Soviet Union. Disregard, if you will, the historical

background as to how that particular regime came to power in the early Twentieth

Century, because the point of this chapter is to assess the compatibility of

economic and political structures. With the Soviets, political power was

effectively concentrated into the hands of a single person. Yes, that person was

elected by the so-called all-powerful "Communist" Party, but once he had settled

into office the fate of the country rested in his hands.

Soviet political power was anything but democratic, it was tyrannical by nature. The economic structure that was attempted, however, was socialist and claimed to be aimed at the Marxist goal of developing a communist state. This is where the mismatch occurs, as socialism is modeled for the benefit of all as nurtured by a receptive and wise few; not exactly what a political order organized around the will of a single dictator is primed to deliver. Tyranny can exist for the collective, but it will never produce a communist utopia.

Regarding the odd mixture of capitalism and democracy, the best model of analysis that we have in this respect is the American system. Now, it is important to take note of the fact that the economic and political models in practice in the United States are neither purely capitalist nor purely democratic, but it is the most prominent example that we have. In the United States, political power is designed to be derived from the people. Granted, the Framers devised a complicated filter to safeguard against direct rule by popular will, but the point of what they created was to have a government which was representative of the governed.

Economically, the American people are theoretically empowered to strive for individual wealth, but the effect of capitalism – even a loosely-regulated version thereof - in practice is that the power gets concentrated into the hands of a few who are clever and otherwise fortunate enough to manipulate the system to their benefit. Capitalism may initially provide an opportunity for prosperity for many, but it eventually tailspins into a feeding frenzy of exploitation until a handful of people manage to conquer their competition. In the process of this economic warfare for industrial domination, those seeking more wealth are

impelled to set their sights on the accompanying political system and resolve to

establish an influence in policymaking so as to remove any and all hurdles to their

individualist goals. To put it another way, the wealthy in an economic system such

as which exists in the United States will always strive for total political and

economic power because anything short of such is perceived as a threat to the

unyielding pursuit of having more. For that reason, a collective-oriented political

system such as democracy can never coexist in the long-term with an

individualist-oriented economic system such as capitalism.

Below is a revised version of the political spectrum. Typically, the

standard spectrum shows four quadrants, Collectivist Authoritarian, Collectivist

Libertarian, Individualist Authoritarian, and Individualist Libertarian. What you

see here is a detailed adaptation of that spectrum to demonstrate where each

political and economic system would fit best. In addition to measuring civil

liberties (authoritarian versus libertarian) and the degree of social

interaction/obligation (collectivism versus individualism), this spectrum measures

the degrees of each (for instance, reactionary – or fascist – authoritarianism or

pacifist libertarianism):

Authoritarianism

	Command Socialism	Interventionist Welfarism	
Statism			Corporatism

Reactionary	Collectivist Tyranny	Collectivist Monarchy	Individualist Monarchy	Individualist Tyranny	Reactionary
Cautionary	Bureaucratic Oligarchy	Bureaucratic Aristocracy	Plutocratic Aristocracy	Plutocratic Oligarchy	Cautionary
Collectivism					Individualism
Noninterventionist	Exclusive Democracy	Exclusive Polity	Structured Stratocracy	Liberal Stratocracy	Noninterventionist
Pacifist	Inclusive Democracy	Inclusive Polity	Structured Anarchy	Liberal Anarchy	Pacifist

Communism	Representative Socialism	Populist Welfarism	Capitalism

Libertarianism

Listed within this spectrum are sixteen types of political systems. More specifically, there are two variations of each of the following systems: tyranny, monarchy, oligarchy, aristocracy, stratocracy, polity, anarchy, and democracy. Yes, a polity is a form of democracy – a representative democracy, to be exact -, but the point of separating the two here is to clarify that a polity is a separate form of governance altogether and that what is meant – here, at least – by "democracy" is a pure or "direct" democratic government model. Getting into the details, one ought to examine the differences between one part of the spectrum and another.

Let's begin with the reactionary authoritarian section of the spectrum. Here is where the concentration of political power tends to dwell in the hands of one person. With fewer minds assessing the conditions of life and pondering the consequences of policies made the more prone to reckless and misguided decisions a governing body becomes. When presided over by a collectivist tyrant, the economic model which accompanies such is statism; which is defined as a system where the people theoretically have total control over their economy, but receive little or no benefits from such. Decentralizing power by a degree – from a reactionary system to a cautionary one – only slightly weakens the statist model under bureaucratic oligarchy in one of a few paths toward communism.

The collectivist monarch enjoys influence over what's called a command socialist economy. He or she is considered to be more attuned to the needs of their people – thereby making their rule "legitimate", according to Aristotle -, and tends to be less extreme in the utilization of their power. On the accompanying economic model, what separates command socialism from representative socialism (which exists under collectivist libertarianism) is the fact that the governed have theoretical control over their economy, but only through the unelected government of either the one or the few. Here, it is possible for the benefits of economic production to be shared by all, but the reality is that the powerful are less likely to fulfill on the promise of socialism since they are relatively unaccountable compared to their democratic counterparts.

Traditionally, most monarchs have been on the individualist end of the spectrum and have been accompanied by interventionist welfarism. An interventionist welfare state is not unlike what the United States presently has. For the most part, the state leaves the market to its own devices, but will occasionally intervene in the interest of averting economic decline. This model of society has largely been abandoned in the Western World with the end of feudalism.

The individualist tyrant is all too common in history and thrives with a corporatist economic regime. Here, greed is perceived to be the end all be all of human existence. The eventual by-product of a society driven purely by selfishness is the concentration of wealth and political power in the hands of a single person or entity at the expense of all. Humanity is relegated to mere tools of production and cannon fodder for wars of choice and human rights are dismissed as a secondary concern after the profit motive.

Moving on to cautionary authoritarianism, on the collectivist end we first see the bureaucratic oligarchs. Political power is concentrated into the hands of a few, but their authority is deemed illegitimate by the rules of Aristotle since the interests of the governed do not take precedence in any decisions. Arguably, the Soviet Union – except when it was ruled by Stalin, at which point it was primarily a tyrannical form of government built in his image – as well as China's "communist" government are examples of bureaucratic oligarchs. In fact, the collapse of the Soviet Union at the end of the Cold War left the people of Russia with a disastrous transition from this form of oligarchy to another which will be discussed later.

Arguably the least dreadful of any authoritarian model is the bureaucratic aristocracy. Accompanied by command socialism, this Aristotelian legitimate governing approach is exactly the type of government which Aristotle and Plato believed to be the perfect design. Decisions are made by highly-"qualified" "philosopher-kings" in the best interest of all. Of course, this was a classical era

utopian dream that never came to fruition and would be a misfit in the modern

world given the drift towards democracy.

Moving across the spectrum's divide into the individualist section,

bureaucracy is replaced by plutocracy. First, accompanied by an interventionist

welfare state is the plutocratic aristocracy. Plutocracy – contrary to the purposes of

bureaucracy – rules in the interests of wealth. The plutocratic aristocrat would be a

"highly qualified", yet unelected, member of a government which makes wise

decisions geared towards enhancing the wealth of a few. As for the economic

model – requiring the occasional government intervention with welfarism -, the

aristocrats here would abide by the rules of basic Keynesian economics in order to

prevent an economic collapse and to curtail revolution.

Under plutocratic oligarchy, corporatism is the dominant economic

model. This is roughly the society which emerged in Russia after the Soviet Union

fell. Power belonged to the wealthy and was exercised purely in accordance

therewith regardless of the consequences. Corruption also runs rampant –

primarily in the form of crony capitalism -, and dissension is likely to produce an

upheaval. To summarize, this model has little hope for prolonged survival since

factionalism – motivated by greed – overwhelms the system and eventually forces

a transition towards a neighboring design and it appears now that this is the case

with Russia.

Shifting across the border into libertarian territory, we first examine the

collectivist noninterventionists. The least collectivist variation here is the exclusive polity. Supported by representative socialism, this model is the slightly more democratic cousin of the "philosopher-king" model preferred by Aristotle and his teacher. The polity under this regime consists only of elitists, typically chosen by upper class members of society; not too different from the original design of America's democracy. As for the economic accompanying model, the socialist approach is meant to reflect the needs of the populace, with popular feedback having a primary influence.

The most collectivist approach in this section finds an exclusive democracy accompanied by a weak version of communism. Politically, power rests in the hands of an elitist or societally-preferred group of citizens, such as with Athenian democracy in its enfranchisement of only male citizens. Since political power is not all-inclusive the economic product is weaker than it ought to be; hence the labeling of its communist economy as "weak". Given the advancements in education and the flow of information, this particular approach has expired in its usefulness for modern humanity.

Now, with individualist noninterventionists, we move to the liberal stratocracy. Built largely through Social Darwinism – where the fittest in society manage to achieve some degree of loose political power, primarily through a demonstration of their strategic military skill as well as a skilled accumulation of wealth -, the accompanying economic model is laissez-faire capitalism. This particular structure for society was more common in an era when humanity was scattered about in small tribes. Decisions for the governed are made by the mighty and are usually for the benefit thereof.

The least individualist model in this respect is the structured stratocracy. Political power is less volatile, as a strict chain of command is erected to protect the order from excessive and disruptive struggles for control. Economically, the model is a populist welfare state where charity for the needy is encouraged but not forced. In this model, one could potentially see the building blocks for a feudal state.

With the individualist pacifists, there exists anarchy. While history has associated anarchy with "left-wing" politics up until now, the important distinction made in this theory between anarchy and communism is that the latter – as you'll soon see – relies on collective strength, whereas anarchy seeks to leave every individual to their own devices. Another key change in how we think about anarchy and communism in the accompaniment theory is that communism is purely perceived to be an economic model whereas anarchy here is deemed to be a political model. Remembering these modified viewpoints going forward will be very helpful in deciphering what is the best course for humanity.

The least individualist approach to pacifism on this end of the spectrum is the structured anarchist model. As is the case with structured stratocracy, structured anarchy is accompanied by a populist welfare state. However, the welfare state in this respect is actually a degree weaker since there is relatively little or no organization to ascertain that the needs of others are addressed. Another crucial point with structured anarchy is that the "structure" comes in the form of loosely-established rules of engagement among individuals: think of how the so-called "Wild West" functioned – at least in the popularized myths - in order to get an idea for how things would work here.

Onward to the most individualist of pacifists, and you find liberal – or "total" – anarchy. Another appropriate description of this political structure would be anocracy, since there is no central government. Accompanied by the purest form of laissez-faire capitalism, liberal anarchy permits a true "every man for himself" society. Theoretically, each person would be free to pursue whatever their heart desired without any strings attached. In reality, since human selflessness is not nurtured to maturity under an individualist society, the completely "liberal" – that is, in the classic meaning of the word – design leaves most people to suffer exploitation and inhumane treatment for the selfish benefit of their more cunning neighbors. Liberal anarchy is not a stable approach because it creates a tremendous imbalance in wealth and access to essential resources, thereby paving the path to a revolution to concentrate economic and/or political power in some way.

Collectivist pacifists represent the most progressive human societies. First off, there is the inclusive polity. A truly representative democracy that is open to all willing participants. Anyone can vote and anyone can seek elective office in this form of government. Economically, the system is representative socialism, which effectively means that all decisions affecting the people's economy are considerate of the effects that will be wrought on the people. Popular input for every decision – economic or otherwise – is seen as crucial. "Command" is placed in the hands of the many through the men and women they elect. This particular model is close to what one sees when looking at most advanced democracies in the modern world; especially throughout Europe.

Lastly, there is the inclusive democracy; in other words, democracy in its purest form. Every citizen of an appropriate age is empowered with a say and all decisions are made with the collective's interests in mind. Furthermore, the accompanying economic model is communism in its purest form. Political and economic participation are seen as everyone's civic duty, with everyone contributing what they can in order to justify the degree to which they benefit from such. This system has never existed, but it was undoubtedly what Karl Marx had in mind when he envisioned a utopian society.

Over the course of human history, society has evolved from our primal hunter-gatherer state to the collection of pseudo-capitalist, mixed, and statist nations you see today. In the beginning, when humanity was in the process of separating itself from the rest of the animal kingdom, our ancestors were heavily reliant on hunting and gathering. Not unlike our fellow earthly inhabitants, early humankind traveled in small groups in accordance with the availability of food, water, and shelter in addition to other concerns pertaining to security. Initially, leadership was either missing or not necessary, since the only real decisions being made for the small group pertained to their periodic movements from one base to another.

This, the original human society, was perhaps the closest functioning example of liberal anarchy that our species will ever experience. Even so, the individual was never left completely alone to survive or starve purely on their own strengths, as the community spirit of his or her fellow travelers no doubt

compelled them to work collectively. Eventually, though, after most of our

existence was dominated by these hunter-gatherers, the evolution of society led to

the formation of leadership roles within each clan and gave rise to the first

chiefdoms. Then, with the arrival of leaders came a unified purpose for each

group, which inevitably created a competition for resources and paved the way for

agriculture.

When humanity mastered the elements and learned how to either

manipulate or capitalize on such to produce enough food and protection for

permanent settlements, we were liberated from our primal need to endlessly scour

the Earth for the essentials of survival. It was at this stage where our species

finally broke away from all others in the animal kingdom. We became masters of

our own destiny, but we also set up an array of new challenges. Soon, greed

supplanted survival and that undoubtedly begat an atmosphere of conflict.

No longer were we satisfied with finding enough food and sufficient

shelter to live another day. No, agriculture ensured that we would never want

again so long as we managed our resources appropriately. Instead, our basic

instincts being accommodated freed us to yearn for more…to yearn for it all. Out

of this war of wealth came the emergence of humanity's next phase: feudalism.

Initially, the shift towards a feudal society came in the form of liberal and

structured stratocracies. Here, the most skilled warriors accumulated power and

began to establish an order wherein an exchange of resources and wealth occurred

between vassals and lords. Over time this society evolved into a plutocratic aristocracy and even further into an individualist or collectivist monarchy in some

cases. The concentration of economic and political power occurred at an

accelerated rate, laying the foundation for the war-ridden era we now know as the

Middle Ages.

Since power in every respect was gravitating in the direction of a few or

one beneficiaries, the quality of life and propensity for oppression also became an

issue. The free exchange of ideas was mostly discouraged if not outright

forbidden. A strict pledge of loyalty to the rule of men – not law - was promoted.

Finally, this focus on centralized power aided in the wealthy rulers' pursuit of

foreign riches via mercantilism and the first era of imperialism.

Greed is an all-powerful force, and when the monarchs and aristocrats of

Europe determined in the 17th Century that the wealth of their nations depended on

the precious metal stockpile they possessed, it was all too clear what they needed

to do next. Empires had existed in the past, but usually it had been for glory's sake

or to establish a dominant legacy. Seeking out the riches of other nations in order

to enhance your own – and, in this respect, the ruling class was never concerned

for a collective benefit of staking claim to foreign wealth as they served

themselves alone when they purportedly did things for the sake of their "nation" –

became the new mission statement of the world's major powers at that time. All

interaction with outsiders was geared towards maximizing the state's wealth,

whether in facilitating trade or in declaring war.

Regarding the latter, the tool of war, the objective was never to "keep the

peace" or to "restore" such, but rather to set up a colony from which to extract riches. This was the original gold standard, and the exploitation of Earth's poorest

inhabitants could not have been worse. More souls than anyone can count slipped

into slavery, entire cultures went extinct, and it was all done in the name of turning

the planet into a massive mine. Seeing this barbarism for what it was left a number

of well-meaning minds with a foul taste in their mouths and inspired them to

envision a different world.

Adam Smith believed - correctly - that a nation's government ought not

to focus its energy on panning the globe for gold to steal and hoard. Instead, he felt

that the government could do a better job by leaving the exploitation of resources

to the individual. A person's free creativity in conjunction with a strong

competitive field involving other creative individuals was believed to be the best

means by which to increase a nation's wealth. This was the vision for capitalism.

Approximately a century later, another mind came into the scene. Karl

Marx contemplated the history of humanity and how the connection between the

economy, the exploitation of labor as well as natural resources, and the fate of

society were inextricable. For Marx, increasing a nation's wealth was not as

crucial to the strength thereof as the fair distribution of same said wealth to all

citizens. Contrary to Smith, Marx believed that society was strongest when a

collective – as opposed to individualist – spirit was promoted. In essence, this is

the vision of communism.

When America's Founding Fathers pondered how their new nation

should function, they were dealing with contemporary realities and their limited

knowledge of the time. Capitalism had not yet been fully tested and communism had yet to be conceived as we know it today. Though the colonies they inhabited

would not have existed without the mercantilism that Smith decried, the men who

sought independence from England's Crown were equally determined to cut off

their ties with its economic legacy. Something new was desired and necessary.

One can not blame this handful of leaders in a brand new nation which

was pioneering a revolutionary age shifting the world in the direction of

democracy for not understanding that the political and economic models they were

crafting would be a mismatch. Moreover, they can not be scolded for the

weaknesses they saw in democracy's success at the time. They were right to

distrust decentralized political power at a time when literacy and suffrage largely

remained in the hands of a wealthy few. Neither democracy nor communism

would have succeeded until everyone had equal access to the information they

needed to effectively participate in the system.

At first, democracy and capitalism appeared to be a perfect match. After

all, both exist in the pacifist plane of our political spectrum. The problem is,

however, that capitalism is an individualist creation whereas democracy can not

survive outside of collectivism. A capitalist must only concern himself with the

one he sees in the mirror, whereas democracy demands its participants to replace

the mirror for a window. Conflating the two ensures one thing: a conflict-ridden

society where every man and woman aspires to enrich themselves at the expense

of others while using their democratic vote to the same ends. In other words, no

democracy can survive the selfishness of capitalism.

What is it that we have to do in order to correct our course? Do we permit the system we have now to just collapse upon itself and try to build a better society out of the ashes? Do we attempt to fix what's wrong with the current framework so as to make it work better? Or do we resolve to work together on beginning a long transition to the very society our species deserves? Ultimately, answering this question is up to the people and the path forward can not - and absolutely should not - be forced upon them.

To fully accommodate the needs of humanity, the recommendation of this book is that the people of every nation on Earth first and foremost take action to seize control of their fate. It is not recommended that taking power into proletarian hands occur violently, because a revolution borne out of violence creates more conflict for the future. Rather, the populist revolution which must transpire first should be purely democratic. Organize, demonstrate, lobby relentlessly, vote, and - through peaceful civil disobedience – resist all unjust restrictions on your activity.

Once the power rests in your hands, the next step is to emphasize the importance of education. An adequately informed populace is far more effective at fending off the oppression of a few than a population left to sift through rumors and the plethora of myths propagated by the status quo. Secure the knowledge and you can ascertain the longevity of your political power. Nothing can stand in your way once you possess this precious tool.

Finally, the people must strive to clean up their political system by ridding it of the oligarchic plague. That is to say that the influence of special interests in the political structure must be completely eradicated so as to establish a clear line of communication between the people and their government. Then,

following the guide of the political spectrum and the details thereof provided

within this chapter, the people can steadily steer their policymakers towards

whatever society is preferable to them. With that in mind, in our closing chapter

we will summarize all that has been discussed throughout this book and highlight

the choices before us in the path ahead.

Section Six: Politics

Chapter Twenty: Choosing Our Path

Chapter Twenty: Choosing Our Path

Revolutions are high-risk events. When a transformation is necessitated at any level of human society, the threat of seeing the transition devolve into utter chaos is enormous. Humankind must tread carefully when contemplating how to proceed to a better world for all. Not everyone will agree that a revolution is required, nor will everyone agree on the best means to revolt. It would be recommended that upending the status quo be an all-inclusive process with an absolute tolerance for dissent. Otherwise, we will not produce a freer, more democratic society, but a loathsome despotic one instead.

Prior to hitting the gas and propelling the lot of us into this path, we must first design and construct that path. This preparation for what lies ahead demands a great degree of respect for all the key components. Throughout this book, you've read about each of the building blocks – individual pieces of the six pillars of Unitism – and have been given a chance to assess both the reality we live in today as well as an alternative vision. What remains is for you to reflect on all that you've read and ask yourself if you are ready to rise up and lead the way or if you are content with the present circumstances.

Ultimately, this introspective journey is up to every individual citizen to ponder. While this book's primary theme is promoting the collective's interests, none of this can be accomplished if the individual isn't free to choose their allegiance in one way or the other. No man, woman, or child should ever be forced to partake in a revolution that they don't believe in, and neither should their right to disagree with such ever be denied – overtly or covertly – them. This revolution belongs to all of us or none of us, and the principles of liberty and democracy ought never to be violated for any reason; especially not in the name of advancing an ideological worldview.

Bear in mind that respect for freedom of thought is an essential cornerstone of the aforementioned pillars. These pillars - Politics, Economics, Human Rights, Science, Justice and Security, as well as Accountability (the last of which is the central concern with the issue of money in politics) – are nonnegotiable and can't be cast aside if humanity is to ever move forward as one. In fact, the pillars are universal in their scope for all political theories, as they represent a core concern of molding a successful and truly civilized society. Consider them to be the map for a road not yet paved.

The Politics Pillar simply gives the new system a means to function and this is where the preference for democracy comes in. A just human society can not exist without democracy in any of its forms. Unless the people are empowered to dictate what transpires in their name, they will never be free. The only legitimate form of government is that which the people have sanctioned and in which they are active participants.

Democracy is best for the people, because each of the alternatives represents manipulation of political power for the one, the few, or none. Tyrants and monarchs ultimately serve only themselves. Oligarchs and aristocrats set out to enrich themselves and maintain an oppressive status quo. As for anarchy, nobody wins, as all humanity is either pitted against one another or left to wither on the vine. Only democracies, whether direct or indirect, focus on what's in the collective's interests at all times.

The Economics Pillar provides the system with a set of instructions for the distribution of wealth. Though it is taboo to say, communism and representative socialism offer the only just approach for said distribution. Here, under true communism and socialism as initially envisioned by Karl Marx, the people dictate how the wealth they produce will be used. Likewise, both communism and representative socialism demand the participation of all beneficiaries in some manner – however they can contribute – so as to guarantee just and equal treatment.

Communism – like direct democracy – exists as part of a utopian dream. They may or may not be attainable, but humanity will never know unless there is at least an attempt to achieve such. In the meantime, representative socialism as accompanied by an inclusive polity will suffice. No "great leap" is possible, as attempting to force society to plunge from one system to another invites a collapse of the order as well as risks countless lives. So long as the people are considered the system's most vital component then there is no need to rush the transition.

The Human Rights Pillar is vital for its emphasis on society's core obligations to protect its people. Unless there is an attempt to underscore how valuable the individual truly is, then society will no doubt soon regard each single person as nothing more than a moving part in a grand machine. Making Human Rights a crucial focus must be paramount if we are ever to secure liberty and keep the promise that the economic and political subsystems work for all. It can even be argued that this aspect of Unitism represents its heart and soul.

Devoid of Human Rights, a system is purely guided by the pursuit of power, and that is the path to anarchy or tyranny. Bear in mind that humanity's most essential right is the freedom of conscience. Men and women ought to always have their right to free choice promoted. Closing the door on free thought prevents us from learning and perfecting our society. Without the freedom to think, we do not create, and without creation we cease to evolve.

The Science Pillar provides the tools for understanding the universe and world around us. Also, with science, we innovate and conquer our reality. Let there be no doubt that a life without scientific understanding would have left humanity in a stagnant, even endangered, existence in Africa, Central Asia, and Europe. We have made great strides towards dominating the animal kingdom and even our collective fate thanks to science.

In the future, science will enable us to discover life's unchartered waters. Together, we will explore worlds not yet seen. Together, we will see an end to plagues such as cancer and AIDS. Together, we will save the world from the havoc that our species has wreaked up to this point. Together, science will allow us to save ourselves.

The Justice and Security Pillar reminds us that there are everlasting threats to the peace. No matter how pristine we make the environment and no matter how many opportunities we provide for our neighbors, there will always be the possibility that one person or a group of people are unsatisfied with harmony. Often used in sports is the expression that "the best offense is a good defense", and the same must apply for society overall. We simply have to prepare ourselves for the worst while we hope and work for the best.

Not only should we set out to protect ourselves with every possible contingency against threats to the peace, but we ought to keep in mind that justice requires recognition that even the perpetrators of ill will deserve a fair hearing. This is the primary concern with this particular pillar; the balance of security and liberty. To a degree, this pillar overlaps a little with the Human Rights Pillar, only because we can't prepare for protection without remembering to protect ourselves from overzealousness and blind vigilance. When we are scared for our safety, we tend to lose ourselves in a frantic search for answers and a determination to seek vengeance. It is incumbent upon all free people to never forget the absolute principle of a fair trial and all that such entails, as keeping the promise of unyielding and blind justice is the first defense we have to maintain our security.

The Accountability Pillar, which did not get much discussion at the beginning of this book – though it has been alluded to throughout -, requires a constant surveillance to be kept on the system by an untainted, clear watchful eye. Whose eye, you may ask? The people's, collectively, through a transparent line of communication, with an unbridled exchange of information, and free of the entanglements of money's corruptive influence over our political system. Without accountability, freedom is just a myth that the people can only hope is true.

Keeping the system accountable to the governed requires a number of things. First of all, a strong educational system which adequately informs the young of humankind's history, teaches them about the rights and tools at their disposal, and prepares them to partake in the community. Secondly, a decentralized media with no profit motive or obligations to protect dominant interests so as to provide for an unfiltered flow of current events information. Finally, to keep the system accountable, the people must have full access to all information pertaining to what their government is doing and their must be an equally open access to said government so that the people can provide feedback; including an elections process which removes the barriers of money, thereby liberating candidates and ideas to be shared with the people for their informed consideration.

We know what we want and we know how we got here. Ahead lies a set of options and the people must make a choice. Will we choose a future of greater unity or continued division? It is up to us to ascertain that the former is made more appealing. We can not accomplish victory simply be demonizing the status quo or by pointing out all its follies. No, humanity requires hope to inspire a meaningful and lasting change.

If we fail to instill a spirit of promise, then the future is left to despair. We've already seen where fear takes our species. From one example to the next throughout human history, fear has toppled one regime in favor of chaos which produces another repugnant regime's erection. When fear motivates revolt, innocent lives are lost for nothing but selfish enrichment. However, when mutual compassion drives the movement, a strong union is created with an enduring mission to lift all out of the abyss of desperation.

To enable the revolution we need, exploitation must become a thing of the past. We must resolve that no human and no resource will be utilized without justification and respect for the same. As products of the Earth ourselves, it is incumbent upon humankind to regard this planet and its many limitations as a partner in our advancement, not simply as an object for us to drain in the name of its most dominant species. Likewise, all other nonhuman inhabitants must be treated with dignity, hunted only when necessary and with respect for the balance necessitated by nature so as to maintain order. Humans do not live here in isolation, for our community ought to extend beyond our kind.

As has been the theme throughout this book, all human beings should be viewed equally. The American Christian White Man is no more valuable than the Cambodian Buddhist Woman. Each is a citizen of Earth, and each requires the other for survival. In the decades and centuries to come, these two individuals will need one another more than they have ever before, as the challenges which await us will impact all.

Our future is rife with global crises and can not be addressed by any single nation or culture. Rather, the greatest threat to humanity is our disunity. Until we see that the answer is to come together and work as one, our responses to the global dangers of income inequality, racism, climate change, education, war, terrorism, healthcare, starvation, and etcetera will always be insufficient. While the future must lead to union, the beginning of this journey starts with you.

Your apprehensions about thinking in global terms must first be addressed. No one but you can confront this challenge. What you must do first is consider your place in the world by looking at such in the following way: how you interact with your neighbors, how your neighborhood interacts with the city or town you call home, how your locale interacts with its region (or, state, in American terms), how your region interacts with your nation, and how your nation interacts with the world. What are you, the individual, doing to influence this interaction? How does the world influence you? What are you willing to do to improve this interaction?

It is natural to fear change. Change is unsettling because it forces us to adapt all over again. All of natural history has consisted of a series of disruptions – whether desired or not – which has required a re-adaptation for the affected living things. No animal or plant enjoys all of these changes, but they are inevitable. What is being promoted here, though, is a change that we can control…and for the better. As masters of our own destiny, the human species has a unique ability here on Earth to shape our evolution. Yes, the past experiences of our ancestors – both human and not - to the transformations that brought us here have primed us to hate change, but things are different. We don't have to fear it anymore.

Choose the path you yearn for yourself, for your children, and for your grandchildren's grandchildren. Would you like them to live the life that you and your forefathers have? Or, can you envision a better world where they are seen as equals, where their fears are largely kept at bay, where their needs are met, and where peace thrives? Don't permit your optimism to be polluted with the established propaganda's claim that such is unattainable. It is entirely up to you – at first – to decide what is attainable before then seeking to attain such.

Let not your positive imagination be stifled with the naysayers' admonitions of doom and gloom. They choose not to dream of a better way and not to partake in the production thereof. They are content with a stagnant – or even declining – human existence dependent on selfish aims. They are willful servants of the few who benefit from the fruits of your toils and the toils of the millions who've come before you.

A revolution can not occur without your consent and wholehearted participation. No, you are an essential part of the movement which must come and push back against the forces of resentment, exploitation, and exclusion. Without you, democracy dies, the community collapses, and anarchy is a certainty. Furthermore, if anarchy is certain, then its instability and the repeated pattern of societal evolution which follows are as well.

Order is a required factor of nature. In the universe, order is maintained by interstellar relativity and the laws of gravity. Among humans, order is demanded to provide that the essentials for mutual survival are guaranteed. Once that guarantee falters, the system collapses and nature takes course to correct the flaw. Presently, we are witnessing an impending collapse due to the inability of the present order to sustain itself. So, humanity is in dire need of another reset, and it is up to us – collectively, and with your help – to guide the coming revolution.

A great deal is at stake as we ponder the question of our individual roles in this transition. Without unity, we risk losing ground in the advancement of science. Without unity, we risk exacerbating the inequality among us. Without unity, we risk a world of worsening warfare and hatred. Without unity, we risk the lives of billions as food and water shortages, accompanied by increasing mortality

rates, are enhanced due to ignoring the threats posed by climate change and

overpopulation on our already strained resources. Without unity, humanity's future

is very much in question.

Contemplate the potential leaps that a united humankind can offer.

United, we could not only slow down climate change, but learn how to adapt to it.

United, we could secure a lasting peace and relegate terrorism to a footnote.

United, we could ensure that every man, woman, and child has everything that

they will ever need, including a full education so as to completely contribute to the

forward thrust of society. United, there is no limit as to what we can accomplish

and how far our species can go.

Fellow concerned citizen of humanity, a choice has been placed before

you. The case has been made that our present global system is hurdling towards a

collapse and that a revolution is on the horizon; or is perhaps already underway.

The question now is how you will receive and use this information. Will you take

what you've read here and seek to expand your understanding in a journey towards

joining the revolt? Or, will you simply dismiss all that has been argued in this

book and go about living life as if nothing needs to be changed?

If the former is what you decide upon and if you are hungry for action,

then there is a list of tasks for you to tackle. For starters, help spread the word

about this movement by sharing this book and all other related materials.

Secondly, don't stop with what you've read here, but rather make it your duty to

absorb more information to fully equip yourself with the intellectual firepower that you will need to be an effective and formidable revolutionary. Afterwards, take to the streets, go door to door, and discuss the revolution with your friends, family, coworkers, and neighbors. Finally, pledge yourself to the cause of enhancing the people's power by swearing or affirming your loyalty to liberty, justice, and democracy above all.

The revolution is inevitable, and it is best that we – the working class of the world – prepare ourselves to take the reins of this stampeding transformation so that we are not trampled underneath. Our future can be one of equal liberty and shared prosperity. We can seize the moment to project our hopes and dreams onto the society in which we live. Working as one, humanity can end much of our suffering and can meet any challenge laid down at our feet. All that we have to do is believe and struggle for this world and it will come to be. No single champion will bring us the utopia we desire. As another great activist of the people once said: "we are the ones we've been waiting for".

Brothers and sisters, the time to unite has come.

The Pillars of Unitism
283

www.ingramcontent.com/pod-product-compliance
Lightning Source LLC
Chambersburg PA
CBHW062130280526
45788CB00001B/118